All
Stitched
Up

Also compiled by Alie Stibbe and published by Monarch:

Bursting at the Seams (with Killy John)

All Stitched Up

Wit and wisdom for today's woman

compiled by
Alie Stibbe

MONARCH
B O O K S
Oxford, UK & Grand Rapids, Michigan, USA

First published in the UK in 2005 by Monarch Books
(a publishing imprint of Lion Hudson plc),
Mayfield House, 256 Banbury Road, Oxford OX2 7DH
Tel: +44 (0) 1865 302750 Fax: +44 (0) 1865 302757
Email: monarch@lionhudson.com
www.lionhudson.com

Distributed by:
UK: Marston Book Services Ltd, PO Box 269,
Abingdon, Oxon OX14 4YN
USA: Kregel Publications, PO Box 2607,
Grand Rapids, Michigan 49501

UK ISBN 1 85424 713 1
US ISBN 0 8254 6093 X

British Library Cataloguing Data
A catalogue record for this book is available
from the British Library.

Printed in Great Britain

To Hannah

Acknowledgements

Thank you to all those who have given permission to use material reproduced in this collection. Every effort has been made to trace original copyright holders where required, though in some cases this has proved impossible. We shall be happy to correct such omissions in future editions.

Thank you again to Karen Oberst for permission to use quotes by women published on her wonderful website.

And a special "thank you" to Mark and our children for their patience and encouragement.

Preface

After my husband and his friend had compiled two volumes of wit and wisdom, I noticed that a mere handful of the entries were accredited to women and I began to wonder if a comment I'd heard a *woman* make on TV was not true – that 80% of women have nothing interesting to say. And if this was indeed so, what were the remaining 20% saying, and was it interesting?

These questions coincided with my being shaken into the awareness that language shapes our reality, and that women's reality is difficult to express because language is inherently gendered – with a bias towards the male. The scientist in me began to investigate ... and *Bursting at the Seams* was born in conspiracy with my friend Killy John, albeit under the watchful editorial eyes of our husbands!

Always the glutton for punishment, one foray into the world of women's words was not enough for me – and so *All Stitched Up* evolved over a further year's worth of idle moments redeemed courtesy of the Internet, doctors' waiting rooms, bookshop coffee bars and scouring the daily press in front of satellite sport.

There is wit in this volume, but *All Stitched Up* is more thought-provoking than *Bursting at the Seams*. It is my hope that some of the quotes will inspire and challenge you in the way they have me. Not everything in this volume reflects my personal point of view – that is not the intention of the collection. The intention is to provoke you, to stir you, to wake you up to look at your life and examine what you believe and why.

Hold on tight – this could be a white-knuckle ride, but hopefully with some laughs along the way!

Alie Stibbe
Chorleywood, 2005

Ability

"If you think you can, you can. And if you think you can't, you're right."

Mary Kay Ash

"I can, therefore I am."

Simone Weil

"It is for us to pray not for tasks equal to our powers, but for powers equal to our tasks."

Helen Keller

"When I see the elaborate study and ingenuity displayed by women in the pursuit of trifles, I feel no doubt of their capacity for the most Herculean undertakings."

Julia Ward Howe

"They can because they think they can."

Virginia Woolf

Acceptance

"Nothing is easy to
the unwilling."
Nikki Giovanni

*"You have to accept whatever
comes and the only important
thing is that you meet it with
courage and with the best you
have to give."*
Eleanor Roosevelt

**"While it is wise to accept what we cannot
change about ourselves, it is also good to remember
that we are never too old to replace discouragement
with bits and pieces of confidence and hope."**
Elaine N Aron
*The Highly Sensitive Person: How to Thrive
When the World Overwhelms You*

Achievement

"The most effective way to
do it, is to do it."
Amelia Earhart

"No set goal achieved satisfies.
Success only breeds a new goal. The
golden apple devoured has seeds. It
is endless."

Bette Davis

*"No matter how far
a person can go, the
horizon is still way
beyond you."*
Zora Neale Hurston

"Every great work, every big accomplishment, has been brought into manifestation through holding to the vision, and, often just before the big achievement, comes apparent failure and discouragement."

Florence Scovel Shinn

"My mother drew a distinction between achievement and success. She said that achievement is the knowledge that you have studied and worked hard and done the best that is in you. Success is being praised by others, and that's nice, too, but not as important or satisfying. Always aim for achievement and forget about success."

Helen Hays

The mathematics of high achievement

Begin with a dream.
DIVIDE the problems and conquer them one by one.
MULTIPLY the exciting possibilities in your mind.
SUBTRACT all the negative thoughts to get started.
ADD enthusiasm and determination.
And the RESULT will be the attainment of your goal.

Anon

"Act as if it were impossible to fail."
Dorothea Brande

"I have long since come to believe that people never mean half of what they say, and that it is best to disregard their talk and judge only their actions."
Dorothy Day
The Long Loneliness

"Great thoughts speak only to the thoughtful mind, but great actions speak to all mankind."
Emily P Bissell

"I've arrived at this outermost edge of my life by my own actions. Where I am is thoroughly unacceptable. Therefore, I must stop doing what I've been doing."
Alice Killer
An Unknown Woman

"In a world where there is so much to be done, I felt strongly impressed that there must be something for me to do."
Dorothea Dix

Remember, people will judge you by your actions, not your intentions. You may have a heart of gold – but so does a hard-boiled egg.
Anon

"One kernel is felt in a hogshead; one drop of water helps to swell the ocean; a spark of fire helps to give light to the world. None are too small, too feeble, too poor to be of service. Think of this and act."

Hannah Moore

"You ask me why I do not write something ... I think one's feelings waste themselves in words; they ought all to be distilled into actions and into actions which bring results."

Florence Nightingale
in Cecil Woodham-Smith, *Florence Nightingale*

Adversity

"Adversity does teach who your real friends are."

Lois McMaster Bujold
A Civil Campaign

"A wounded deer leaps the highest."

Emily Dickinson

"If we had no winter, the spring would not be so pleasant: if we did not sometimes taste of adversity, prosperity would not be so welcome."

Anne Bradstreet
Meditations Divine and Moral

"It is very difficult to live among people you love and hold back from offering them advice."

Anne Tyler
Celestial Navigation

"Ask advice only of your equals."

Danish proverb

"If I were asked to give what I consider the single most useful bit of advice for all humanity it would be this: Expect trouble as an inevitable part of life and when it comes, hold your head high, look it squarely in the eye and say, 'I will be bigger than you. You cannot defeat me.'"

Ann Landers

"People are always willing to follow advice when it accords with their own wishes."

Marguerite, Lady Blessington
The Confessions of an Elderly Lady

"Do not ask for fulfilment in all your life, but for patience to accept frustration. Do not ask for perfection in all you do, but for the wisdom not to repeat mistakes. Do not ask for more, before saying 'thank you' for what you have already received."

Brenda Short

"As time passes we all get better at blazing a trail through the thicket of advice."

Margot Bennett

"If I had to give one piece of advice to my daughter on living a happy and successful life, it would be to say, 'No!' And as often as she wants to. I didn't say 'No!' enough."

Isabella Rossellini
Woman & Home, July 2003

Some Advice to Consider?

It's always darkest before dawn. So if you're going to steal the neighbour's newspaper, that's the time to do it.

Never test the depth of the water with both feet.

It may be that your sole purpose in life is simply to serve as a warning to others.

If you think nobody cares if you're alive, try missing a couple of car payments.

If you tell the truth you don't have to remember anything.

If you lend someone £20, and never see that person again, it was probably worth it.

Some days you are the fly; some days you are the windscreen.

If at first you don't succeed, skydiving is not for you.

Never ask a hairdresser if she thinks you need a haircut.

To the world you might be one person, but to one person you might be the world.

Going to church does not make you a Christian any more than going to McDonald's makes you a hamburger.

A coincidence is when God performs a miracle,
and decides to remain anonymous.

Sometimes the majority only means that all the fools
are on the same side.

*Life is like an onion: you peel off one layer
at a time and sometimes you weep.*

*Learn from the mistakes of others.
You can't live long enough to make them all yourself.*

Following the path of least resistance is what
makes rivers and men crooked.

**Life is 10% what happens to you,
and 90% how you respond to it.**

Alge

The Senility Prayer

God, grant me the senility to forget the people I never liked anyway,
the good fortune to run into the ones that I do,
and the eyesight to tell the difference.

Source unknown

Now that I'm older, here's what I've discovered:

I started out with nothing, and I still have most of it.

I finally got my head together; now my body is falling apart.

Funny, I don't remember being absent-minded ...

If all is not lost, where is it?

It is easier to get older than it is to get wiser.

I wish the buck stopped here; I sure could use a few.

Kids in the back seat cause accidents. Accidents in the back seat cause ... kids.

It's hard to make a comeback when you haven't been anywhere.

The only time the world beats a path to your door is when you're in the bathroom.

It's not hard to meet expenses ... they're everywhere.

These days, I spend a lot of time thinking about the hereafter ... I go somewhere to get something, and then wonder what I'm hereafter.

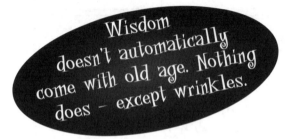

Wisdom doesn't automatically come with old age. Nothing does – except wrinkles.

"Though it sounds absurd, it is true to say I felt younger at 60 than I felt at 20."

Ellen Glasgow
The Woman Within

"It's true, some wines improve with age. But only if the grapes were good in the first place."

Abigail van Buren

"You know you're old when you've lost all your marvels."

Merry Browne

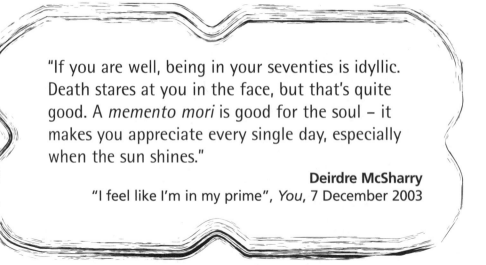

"If you are well, being in your seventies is idyllic. Death stares at you in the face, but that's quite good. A *memento mori* is good for the soul – it makes you appreciate every single day, especially when the sun shines."

Deirdre McSharry
"I feel like I'm in my prime", *You*, 7 December 2003

"It is a mistake to regard age as a downhill grade toward dissolution. The reverse is true. As one grows older, one climbs with surprising strides."

George Sand

"The women who wear their age best are those who remain open to change."

Anne Pitcher
Telegraph Weekend, 21 June 2003

An 80-year-old couple were having problems remembering things, so they decided to go to their doctor to get checked out to make sure nothing was wrong with them.

When they arrived at the doctor's, they explained to him the problems they were having with their memory. After checking the couple out, the doctor told them that they were physically OK but might want to start writing things down and making notes to help them remember things. The couple thanked the doctor and left.

Later that night while watching TV, the old man got up from his chair. His wife asked, "Where are you going?"

"To the kitchen," he replied.

"Will you get me a bowl of ice cream?" she asked.

"Sure," he replied.

"Don't you think you should write it down so you can remember it?"

"No," he said. "I can remember that."

"Well," said his wife, "I would also like some strawberries on top. You'd better write that down because I know you'll forget that."

"I can remember that!" came the response. "You want a bowl of ice cream with strawberries."

"Well, I would *also* like whipped cream on top. I know you'll forget that so you'd better write it down."

With irritation in his voice, the old man said, "I don't need to write that down. I can remember that."

He fumed into the kitchen. After about 20 minutes he returned from the kitchen and handed his wife a plate of bacon and eggs. She stared at the plate for a moment and said, "You forgot my toast."

"Let me advise you not to talk of yourself as being old. There is something in Mind Cure, after all, and if you continually talk of yourself as being old, you may perhaps bring on some of the infirmities of age. At least I would not risk it if I were you."

Hannah Whitall Smith

"It makes sense to me to prepare for old age and find ways of making it exciting for myself."

Sheila Hancock
Interview, *Radio Times*,
13–19 December 2003

"Years are only garments, and you either wear them with style all your life, or else you go dowdy to the grave."

Dorothy Parker

"I never feel age …
If you have creative work, you don't
have age or time."

Louise Nevelson

"We grow
neither better
nor worse as we
get old, but
more like
ourselves."
May Lamberton Becker

"Surely the consolation prize of age is finding out how few things are worth worrying over, and how many things that we once desired, we don't want any more."

Dorothy Dix

Ageing

"I have a problem about being nearly 60: I keep waking up in the morning and thinking I'm 31."

Elizabeth Janeway
Between Myth and Morning

"Jesus, please teach me to appreciate what I have, before time forces me to appreciate what I had."

Susan L Lenzkes

"Youth is the time of getting, middle age of improving, and old age of spending."

Anne Bradstreet

"You can stay young as long as you can learn, acquire new habits and suffer contradiction."

Marie von Ebner-Eschenbach

"I look forward to being older, when what you look like becomes less and less an issue and what you are is the point."

Susan Sarandon

"All I want is to grow old with dignity and calm, without desperation and the need to hang on to stardom."

Jamie Lee Curtis
Daily Telegraph, 20 December 2003

You Might be a Child of the 80s If ...

You have deep, personal relationships via computers with people you've never met in real life before.

The phrase "going courting", to you, means fighting an unjust traffic ticket or playing tennis.

The *Brady Bunch* movie brought back cool memories.

A predominant colour in your childhood photos is "plaid".

You see teenagers today wearing clothes that show up in those childhood photos, and they still look bad.

You remember when music that was labelled "alternative" really was.

You can't remember when the word "networking" didn't have a computer connotation to it as well.

You took family trips before the invention of the mini-van. You rode in the back of the station wagon and you faced the cars behind you.

You've recently horrified yourself by using any one of the following phrases:
> "When I was younger"
> "When I was your age"
> "You know, back when ... "
> "Because I said so, that's why"
> "What is this noise on the radio?"
> "Just can't (fill in the blank) like I used to"

You can't remember a time when "going out for coffee" didn't involve 49,000 selections to choose from.

Kids that work in restaurants and supermarkets annoy you by calling you "sir" or "ma'am".

"Celebration" by Kool & the Gang was one of the hot new songs when you first heard it at a school dance.

You freaked out when you found that you now fall into the "26–50" age category on most questionnaires.

Your hair, at some point in time in the 80s, became something which can only be described by the phrase "I was experimenting".

You're starting to believe (now that it wouldn't affect you) that maybe having the kids go to school year-round wouldn't be such a bad idea after all.

You're doing absolutely nothing with anything pertaining to your major degree.

You want to go out dancing, you really, really do, but your back hurts, sorry.

You're finding that you just don't understand more than half the lingo used on MTV any more.

U2 is too "popular" and "mainstream" for you now.

When someone mentions two consecutive days of the week, the *Happy Days* theme is stuck in your head for hours on end.

You spend endless nights dreaming about being the *Bionic Woman* or *Wonder Woman* or the *Six Million Dollar Man*.

You know who shot JR.

This rings a bell: "My name ... is Charlie. They work for me."

Aims

"If you can't do what you want, do what you can."
Lois McMaster Bujold
Memory

"What we truly and earnestly aspire to be, that in some sense, we are. The mere aspiration, by changing the frame of the mind, for the moment realises itself."
Anna Jameson

"Set your sights high, the higher the better. Expect the most wonderful things to happen, not in the future but right now."
Eileen Caddy

Alcohol

"You are not as bright as you feel after the second drink."
Peggy Bracken

If you know someone who tries to drown their sorrows, you might tell them sorrows know how to swim.
Anon

One tequila, two tequila, three tequila, floor …

Chemistry class

A chemistry teacher wanted to teach her Year 6 class a lesson about the evils of drinking alcohol, so she produced an experiment that involved a glass of water, a glass of whisky and two worms.

"Now, class, observe closely the worms," said the teacher, putting the first worm into the water. It swam about, happy as a worm in water could be.

The second worm, she put into the whisky. It writhed painfully and quickly sank to the bottom, dead as a doornail.

"Now, what lesson can we derive from this experiment?" the teacher asked.

Little Anna raised her hand and wisely responded, "Drink whisky and you won't get worms!"

(NB Don't try this — it's cruel to worms!)

Alone

"To be alone is to be different, to be different is to be alone."
Suzanne Gordon
Lonely in America

"Any woman who accepts aloneness as the natural by-product of success is accepting the punishment for a crime she didn't commit."
Marlo Thomas

"Anything you fully do is an alone journey."
Natalie Goldberg

"The person who tries to live alone will not succeed as a human being. His heart withers if it does not answer another heart. His mind shrinks away if he hears only the echoes of his own thoughts and finds no other inspiration."

Pearl S Buck

Ambition

"I always wanted to be somebody. If I made it, it's half because I was game enough to take a lot of punishment along the way and half because there were a lot of people who cared enough to help me."

Althea Gibson

"If you have a great ambition, take as big a step as possible in the direction of fulfilling it. The step may only be a tiny one, but trust that it may be the largest one possible for now."

Mildred McAfee

"What I wanted to be when I grew up was – in charge!"
Wilma Vaught,
USAF Brigadier General

Anger

"Anger makes you smaller, while forgiveness forces you to grow beyond what you were."

Cherie Carter-Scott
If Love Is a Game, These Are the Rules

"The more anger towards the past you carry in your heart, the less capable you are of loving in the present."
Barbara De Angelis

"Anger is a signal, and one worth listening to."

Harriet Lerner
The Dance of Anger

"When the habitually even-tempered suddenly fly into a passion, that explosion is apt to be more impressive than the outburst of the most violent amongst us."

Margery Allingham
Death of a Ghost

"The devil sends me so offensive a spirit of bad temper that at times I think I could eat people up."
St Teresa of Avila

Anxiety

> **"If I knew what I was so anxious about, I wouldn't be so anxious."**
> **Mignon McLaughlin**

"Anxiety is love's greatest killer. It makes others feel as you might when a drowning man holds on to you. You want to save him, but you know he will strangle you with his panic."

Anaïs Nin
The Diary of Anaïs Nin, vol. 4, 1944–1947

Appearance

"If all you have to offer is a look that is supposed to be appealing, then you are going to be paid attention to about a tenth as long as you would be if when you speak you are interesting."

Julia Roberts

"Obsession with one's appearance is embarrassingly adolescent and actually gets quite boring after a while, not to mention time-consuming."

Marian Keyes,
"Mirror, Mirror on the Wall", *Woman & Home*, May 2003

"The most popular image of the female, despite the exigencies of the clothing trade, is all boobs and buttocks, a hallucinating sequence of parabolas and bulges."

Germaine Greer

"If people think I'm a dumb blonde because of the way I look, then they're dumber than they think I am."

Dolly Parton

"The rarest thing in the world is a woman who is pleased with photographs of herself."

Elizabeth Metcalf

"I've had to look at myself in old movies or on album covers ... I really looked good there, and why didn't I know that *then*? Why didn't I appreciate myself?"

Barbra Streisand
Reader's Digest, November 2003

"A woman can look both moral and exciting ... if she also looks as if it was quite a struggle."

Edna Ferber

"A homely face and no figure have aided many women heavenwards."

Minna Antrim

"Never 'just run out for a few minutes' without looking your best. It's not vanity – it's self-liking."

Estée Lauder

Attitude

"A strong,
positive attitude
will create more
miracles than any
wonder drug."
Patricia Neal

"Could we change our
attitude, we should not
only see life differently,
but life itself would come
to be different."
Katherine Mansfield

Babies

"Babies never extend any credit. They have a tyrant's disdain for fairness. They grant no time off for cuddles received, no parole for long hours nursing in the dark. You can answer that cry a hundred times and on the 101st they'll still have you court-martialled for desertion."

Allison Pearson
I Don't Know How She Does It

Three American Indian women are sitting side by side. The first, sitting on a goatskin, has a son who weighs 170 pounds. The second, sitting on a deerskin, has a son who weighs 130 pounds. The third, seated on a hippopotamus hide, weighs 300 pounds.

What famous theorem does this illustrate?

Naturally, the answer is that the squaw on the hippopotamus is equal to the sons of the squaws on the other two hides.

Beauty

"Beautiful young people are accidents of nature, but beautiful old people are works of art."
Marjorie Barstow Breenbie

"I believe that no woman is so devoid of charms that she cannot make herself attractive along the lines of whatever is most characteristically herself."
Helena Rubenstein

"No one looks as beautiful as a cover girl. It's impossible."
Cindy Crawford
Good Housekeeping,
September 2003

"A mode of conduct, a standard of courage, discipline, fortitude, and integrity can do a great deal to make a woman beautiful."
Jacqueline Bisset

"In this country it's not done to be pretty and clever … men think you're scary and some silly women think you're after their husbands."
Annabel Giles
Red, October 2003

"Those who don't enjoy their own spirit, sensuality, personality, and preferences are never as beautiful as they could be."
Regina Thomashauer

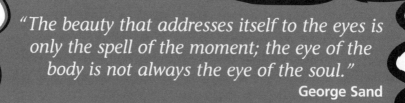

"The beauty that addresses itself to the eyes is only the spell of the moment; the eye of the body is not always the eye of the soul."
George Sand

"To seek after beauty as an end is a wild-goose chase, a will-o'-the wisp, because it is to misunderstand the very nature of beauty, which is the normal condition of a thing being as it should be."

Ade Bethune

"Beauty does not come from creams and lotions. God can give us beauty, but whether that beauty remains or changes is determined by our thoughts and deeds."

Delores Del Rio

A WOMAN'S PRAYER

Now I lay me down to sleep,
I pray the Lord my shape to keep.
Please no wrinkles, please no bags,
And lift my butt before it sags.

Please no age spots, please no grey
And as for my tummy – take it away.
Please keep me healthy, keep me young,
And thank you, Lord, for all you've done.

Anon

Beginnings

"Let us begin afresh every day! The heavier is your burden, the stronger and more courageous should be your heart, fearless of all that may chance to befall you."

St Catherine of Siena

"Don't wait for something big to occur. Start where you are, with what you have, and that will always lead you into something greater."
Mary Manin Morrissey

"We spend January 1st walking through our lives, room by room, drawing up a list of work to be done, cracks to be patched. Maybe this year, to balance the list, we ought to walk through the rooms of our lives … not looking for flaws, but for potential."
Ellen Goodman

"The beginning is always today."
Mary Wollstonecraft Shelley

"Begin doing what you want to do now. We are not living in eternity. We have only this moment, sparkling like a star in our hand and melting like a snowflake. Let us use it before it is too late."
Marie Beyon Ray

Bereavement

"The best consolation after bereavement is family."
Nina Bawden
Saga, August 2003

"One way love begins to heal us is through those who are close to us."
Elaine Storkey
Losing a Child

"Although Time definitely doesn't heal – that's a cliché ripe for slaughter – it does a pretty good job at running repairs."
Helen Osbourne (widow of playwright John Osbourne)
Sunday Telegraph, 29 June 2003

Bible

The following statements about the Bible were written by children. They have not been retouched or corrected (i.e., incorrect spelling has been left in). That's the best part – enjoy!

1. In the first book of the bible, Guinessis, God got tired of creating the world, so he took the Sabbath off.

2. Adam and Eve were created from an apple tree. Noah's wife was called Joan of Ark.

3. Noah built an ark, which the animals came on to in pears.

4. The Jews were a proud people and throughout history they had trouble with the unsympathetic Genitals.

5. Samson was a strongman who let himself be led astray by a Jezebel like Delilah.

6. Samson slew the Philistines with the axe of the Apostles.

7. Moses led the Hebrews to the Red Sea, where they made unleavened bread which is bread without any ingredients.

8. The Egyptians were all drowned in the dessert. Afterwards, Moses went up on Mount Cyanide to get the ten ammendments.

9. The first commandment was when Eve told Adam to eat the apple.

10. The seventh commandment is thou shalt not admit adultery.

11. Moses died before he ever reached Canada. Then Joshua led the Hebrews in the battle of Geritol.

12. The greatest miracle in the Bible is when Joshua told his son to stand still and he obeyed him.

13. David was a Hebrew king skilled at playing the liar. He fought with the Finklesteins, a race of people who lived in Biblical times.

14. Solomon, one of David's sons, had 300 wives and 700 porcupines.

15. When Mary heard that she was the mother of Jesus, she sang the Magna Carta.

16. When the three wise guys from the east side arrived, they found Jesus in the manager.

17. Jesus was born because Mary had an immaculate contraption.

18. St John the blacksmith dumped water on his head.

19. Jesus enunciated the Golden Rule, which says to do one to others before they do one to you. He also explained, a man doth not live by sweat alone.

20. It was a miracle when Jesus rose from the dead and managed to get the tombstone off the entrance.

21. The people who followed the Lord were called the twelve decibels.

22. The epistles were the wives of the apostles.

23. One of the oppossums was St Matthew who was also a taximan.

24. St Paul cavorted to Christianity. He preached holy acrimony, which is another name for marriage.

25. Christians have only one spouse. This is called monotony.

"The Complete Non-standard Bible" from *Fractured English* by Richard Lederer, 1996

"It may not always feel like my best-loved book, exactly, but it remains the one I can least happily do without."
Catherine Fox
"Books we can't live without", *England on Sunday*, 23 October 2003

Short Jokes about the Bible

Q. How did Adam and Eve feel when expelled from the Garden of Eden?
A. *They were really put out.*

Q. How do we know that Job went to a chiropractor?
A. *Because in Job 16:12 we read, "I had come to be at ease, but he proceeded to shake me up and he grabbed me by the back of the neck and proceeded to smash me."*

Q. What do they call pastors in Germany?
A. *German Shepherds.*

Q. What excuse did Adam give to his children as to why he no longer lived in Eden?
A. *Your mother ate us out of house and home.*

Q. What is the best way to get to Paradise?
A. *Turn right and go straight.*

Q. What kind of man was Boaz before he got married?
A. *Ruth-less.*

Q. What kind of motor vehicles are in the Bible?
A. *2 Corinthians 4:8 describes going out in service in a Volkswagen Beetle: "We are pressed in every way, but not cramped beyond movement."*

Q. What kind of motor vehicles are in the Bible?
A. *David's Triumph was heard throughout the land.*

Q. What kind of motor vehicles are in the Bible?
A. *Honda … because the apostles were all in one Accord.*

Q. What kind of motor vehicles are in the Bible?
A. *Jehovah drove Adam and Eve out of the Garden in a Fury.*

Q. Where is the first baseball game in the Bible?
A. *In the big inning, Eve stole first, Adam stole second. Cain struck out Abel, and the Prodigal Son came home. The Giants and the Angels were rained out.*

Q. Where is the first tennis match mentioned in the Bible?
A. *When Joseph served in Pharaoh's court.*

Q. Which area of Palestine was especially wealthy?
A. *The area around the Jordan. The banks were always overflowing.*

Q. Which servant of Jehovah was the most flagrant lawbreaker in the Bible?
A. *Moses. Because he broke all ten commandments at once.*

Q. Who is the greatest babysitter mentioned in the Bible?
A. *David. He rocked Goliath to sleep.*

Q. Who was the greatest comedian in the Bible?
A. *Samson. He brought the house down.*

Q. Who was the greatest female financier in the Bible?
A. *Pharaoh's daughter. She went down to the bank of the Nile and drew out a little prophet.*

Q. Who was the greatest financier in the Bible?
A. *Noah. He was floating his stock while everyone else was in liquidation.*

Q. Why was Goliath so surprised when David hit him with a slingshot?
A. *The thought had never entered his head before.*

Q: What do you call a sleepwalking nun?
A: *A roamin' Catholic!*

Q: When was the longest day in the Bible?
A: *The day Adam was created, because there was no Eve.*

Q: Why did God create man before woman?
A: *He didn't want any advice.*

Q: Why did Moses wander in the desert for 40 years?
A: *Even then, men wouldn't ask for directions!*

Q: Why didn't Noah go fishing?
A: *He only had two worms!*

Q: Why do they say "Amen" at the end of a prayer instead of "Awomen"?
A: *The same reason they sing Hymns instead of Hers!*

Blame

"Life appears to me too short to be spent in nursing animosity or registering wrong."
Charlotte Brontë

"How prone we are to blame others, when we ourselves only are in fault."
Marguerite, Lady Blessington

Blessing

"To bless is to put a bit of yourself into something. It is to make holy, to change something or someone because of your presence."
Macrina Wiederkehr
A Tree Full of Angels

Body

"No matter what you look like, you have to know which bits of you are unique and make the most of them … Everyone has the right to be the size they're happy with and it's terribly sad if people can't be their natural shape."

Toyah Wilcox
Good Housekeeping, September 2003

"Over the years your bodies become walking autobiographies, telling friends and strangers alike of the minor and major stresses of your lives."
Marilyn Ferguson

"The body is a sacred garment."
Martha Graham

"The chief excitement in a woman's life is spotting women who are fatter than she is."
Helen Rowland

"Used to think it was important to be a size 10 … but now I'm older and wider."

Kathy Shaskan
Cartoon caption for "Blossom Fuller"

"I've got my figure back after giving birth. Sad – I'd hoped to get somebody else's."
Caroline Quentin

"You start out happy that you have no hips or boobs. All of a sudden you get them, and it feels sloppy. Then just when you start liking them, they start drooping."

Cindy Crawford

Bravery

"It is better to
die on your feet
than live on
your knees."
Dolores Ibarruri

*"The bravest
thing you can do
when you are not brave
is to profess courage and
act accordingly."*
Corra Harris

Censorship

"Censorship, like charity, should begin at home, but unlike charity, it should end there."

Clare Boothe Luce

*"Censorship is never over for those who have experienced it.
It is a brand on the imagination that affects the individual who has suffered it, forever."*

Nadine Gordimer

"The free expression of the hopes and aspirations of a people is the greatest and only safety in a sane society."

Emma Goldman
Living my Life

Certainty

"I tore myself away from the safe comfort of certainties through my love for the truth; and truth rewarded me."

Simone de Beauvoir

"When all is said and done, the weather and love are the two elements about which one can never be sure."
Alice Hoffman
Here on Earth

"What is important is to keep learning, to enjoy challenge, and to tolerate ambiguity. In the end there are no certain answers."
Martina Horner

Challenge

"Challenge is a dragon
with a gift in its
mouth ... Tame
the dragon and
the gift is yours."
Noela Evans

"Maybe the greatest
challenge now is to find a
way to keep independence
while also committing
ourselves to the ties that
bind people, families, and
ultimately societies
together."

Jane O'Reilly

*"Providence has hidden a charm in
difficult undertakings which is
appreciated only by those who dare to
grapple with them."*

Anne-Sophie Swetchine

Change

*"To realise that the whole of one's life must be open to
the possibility of change asks ... for an open and free
response to the challenges with which God will face us."*
Esther de Waal
Seeking God: The Way of St Benedict

Change is inevitable, except from vending machines.
Anon

"When you're stuck in a spiral, to change all aspects of the spin you need only change one thing."
Christina Baldwin

"That's the risk you take if you change: that people you've been involved with won't like the new you. But other people who do will come along."
Lisa Alther

"Disconnecting from change does not recapture the past. It loses the future."
Kathleen Norris
O Magazine,
January 2004

"Only I can change my life. No one can do it for me."
Carol Burnett

"Neither situations nor people can be altered by the interference of an outsider. If they are to be altered, that alteration must come from within."
Phyllis Bottome
Survival

"To be able to look at change as an opportunity to grow – that is the secret to being happy."
Joan Lunden

Character

"Character – the willingness to accept responsibility for one's own life – is the source from which self-respect springs."

Joan Didion
Slouching Towards Bethlehem

"The real judges of your character aren't your neighbours, your relatives, or even the people you play bridge with. The folks who really know you are waiters, waitresses, and clerks."

Katherine Piper

"Live your life while you have it. Life is a splendid gift. There is nothing small in it. For the greatest things grow by God's law out of the smallest. You must not fritter it away in 'fair purpose, erring act, inconstant will'; but must make your thoughts, your words, your acts, all work to the same end, and that end not self, but God. That is what we call character."

Florence Nightingale

"Character builds slowly, but it can be torn down with incredible swiftness."

Faith Baldwin
"July", *Harvest of Hope*

"It's wonderful to watch a pretty woman with character grow beautiful."

Mignon McLaughlin
The Second Neurotic's Notebook

"The farther behind I leave the past, the closer I am to forging my own character."

Isabelle Eberhardt

Cheerfulness

"Cheerfulness, it would appear, is a matter which depends fully as much on the state of things within, as on the state of things without and around us."
Charlotte Brontë

Childbirth

THE COUNTRY DOCTOR

An old country doctor went way out to the backwoods to deliver a baby. It was so far out, there was no electricity. When the doctor arrived, no one was home except for the labouring mother and her five-year-old child.

The doctor instructed the child to hold a lantern high so he could see while he helped the woman deliver the baby. The child did so, the mother pushed and after a little while, the doctor lifted the newborn baby by the feet and spanked him on the bottom to get him to take his first breath.

The doctor then asked the five-year-old what he thought of the baby.

"Spank him again," the five-year-old said. "He shouldn't have crawled up there in the first place!"

"Childbirth classes neglect to teach one critical skill: how to breathe, count and swear all at the same time."
Linda Filterman

Child-raising

"I will fight for my children on any level so they can reach their potential as human beings and in their public duties."
Princess Diana

"You have no idea of the costs of children until you have them … "
Jane Rootes
Daily Telegraph, 21 November 2003

"We've begun to raise our daughters more like sons … but few have had the courage to raise their sons more like … daughters."
Gloria Steinem

"Childcare is one of the most amazing activities anyone can do, usually harder than other kinds of employment, and hugely responsible."
Claire Foster
"Long hours that might mean love or neglect",
Church Times,
17 October 2003

> "The best things in life aren't free. Statistics show that the cost of raising a child, from birth to 21, is £140,000 – nearly £3,000 more than the price of an average house. Bringing up three children costs parents nearly half a million pounds."
>
> **Sarah Womack**
> *Daily Telegraph*, 21 November 2003

Dear Lord, it's such a hectic day
With little time to stop and pray,
For life's been anything but calm
Since you called on me to be a mum.
Running errands, matching socks,
Building "F" with building blocks,
Cooking, cleaning, and finding shoes
And other stuff that children lose,
Fitting lids on bottled bugs,
Wiping tears and giving hugs,
A stack of last week's mail to read,
So where's the quiet time I need?
Yet when I steal a minute, Lord,
Just at the sink or ironing board
To ask the blessings of your grace,
I see then, in my small one's face,
That you have blessed me
All the while
And I stop to kiss
That precious smile.

"You have to love your children unselfishly. That's hard. But it's the only way."

Barbara Bush

"When you finally accept that you're a complete dork, your life gets easier. There's no sense trying to be cool. Invariably your children will think you're a big loser, so why fight it?"

Reese Witherspoon

"If a child is to keep his inborn sense of wonder,
he needs the companionship of at least one adult who can
share it, rediscovering with him the joy, excitement and
mystery of the world we live in."

Rachel Carson

"In early childhood you may lay the foundation of poverty
or riches, industry or idleness, good or evil, by the habits to which
you train your children. Teach them right habits then,
and their future life is safe."

Lydia Sigourney

*"It goes without saying that you should never have more
children than you have car windows."*

Erma Bombeck

***"I would be the most content if my children grew up to be
the kind of people who think decorating consists mostly of
building enough bookshelves."***

Anna Quindlen

"If you bungle raising your children, I don't think whatever
else you do well matters very much."

Jacqueline Kennedy Onassis

Children

GREAT TRUTHS ABOUT LIFE THAT LITTLE CHILDREN HAVE LEARNED

1. No matter how hard you try, you can't baptise cats.
2. When your mum is mad at your dad, don't let her brush your hair.
3. If your sister hits you, don't hit her back. They always catch the second person.
4. Never ask your three-year-old brother to hold a tomato.
5. You can't trust dogs to watch your food.
6. Don't sneeze when someone is cutting your hair.
7. Never hold a Dust-Buster and a cat at the same time.
8. You can't hide a piece of broccoli in a glass of milk.
9. Don't wear polka-dot underwear under white shorts.
10. The best place to be when you're sad is Grandpa's lap.

"I think having children helps you realise something about God's infinite creativity, because you can't begin to imagine what your own children are going to be like."

Jane Williams
Church of England Newspaper, 18–25 December 2003

"Always be nice to your children – because they are the ones who will choose your rest home."

Phyllis Diller

"Children require guidance and sympathy far more than instruction."

Anne Sullivan

"Children have more need of models than of critics."

Carolyn Coats

"Children are sponges – they copy us."

Lorraine Kelly
Good Housekeeping,
September 2003

"The best thing to spend on your children is your time."
Louise Hart

"What a child doesn't receive he can seldom later give."

P D James
Time to Be in Earnest

"Children are apt to live up to what you believe of them."

Lady Byrd Johnson

"Children in families are like flowers in a bouquet: there's always one determined to face in the opposite direction from the way the arranger desires."

Marcelene Cox

Some Children's Wisdom

"For centuries, people thought the moon was made of green cheese. Then the astronauts found that the moon is really a big hard rock. That's what happens to cheese when you leave it out." (Age 6)

"Think of the biggest number you can. Now add five. Then, imagine if you had that many Twinkies. Wow, that's five more than the biggest number you could come up with!" (Age 6)

"As you make your way through this hectic world of ours, set aside a few minutes each day. At the end of the year, you'll have a couple of days saved up." (Age 7)

"It would be terrible if the Red Cross Bloodmobile got into an accident. No, wait. That would be good because if anyone needed it, the blood would be right there." (Age 5)

Chocolate

One of life's mysteries is how a two-pound box of chocolates can make a woman gain five pounds.

"Don't wreck a sublime chocolate experience by feeling guilty. Chocolate isn't like premarital sex. It will not make you pregnant. And it always feels good."

Lora Brody

The Shopping Bag Law

The bar of chocolate you planned to eat on the way home from the supermarket has somehow hidden itself at the bottom of the shopping bag.

"Anything is good if it is made out of chocolate."

Jo Brand

"As with most fine things, chocolate has its season. There is a simple memory aid that you can use to determine whether it is the correct time to order chocolate dishes: any month whose name contains the letter a, e, or u is the proper time for chocolate."

Sandra Boynton
Chocolate: The Consuming Passion

Choice

"You are in control of your life. Don't ever forget that. You are what you are because of the conscious and subconscious choices you have made."

Barbara Hall
A Summons to New Orleans

"I believe that every single event in life happens as an opportunity to choose love over fear."
Oprah Winfrey

"I am who I choose to be. I always have been what I chose … though not always what I pleased." **Lois McMaster Bujold** *Memory*

"Mankind's greatest gift, also its greatest curse, is that we have free choice. We can make our choices built from love or from fear." **Elisabeth Kübler-Ross**

"We have no choice of what colour we're born or who our parents are or whether we're rich or poor. What we do have is some choice over what we make of our lives once we're here." **Mildred D Taylor**

Clothing

"Clothes and courage have much to do with each other."

Sara Jeanette Duncan

The body is the shell of the soul, and dress the husk of that shell; but the husk often tells what the kernel is.

Anon

"Clothes should never be worn just to hide in … if you're large, people are going to notice you anyway, so why not dress to impress rather than hide your body away?"

Anna Scholz
Good Housekeeping,
September 2003

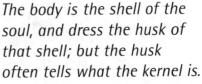

"A dress makes no sense unless it inspires men to want to take it off you."
Françoise Sagan

"You can have anything you want in life if you dress for it."
Edith Head

"Put even the plainest woman into a beautiful dress and unconsciously she will try to live up to it."

Lady Duff-Gordon

"A woman's dress should be like a barbed-wire fence: serve its purpose without obstructing the view."

Sophia Loren

"An ounce of sequins can be worth a pound of home cooking."

Marilyn vos Savant

"Some women hold up dresses that are so ugly and they always say the same thing: 'This looks much better on.' On what? On fire?"

Marsha Warfield

"You don't have to signal a social conscience by looking like a frump. Lace knickers won't hasten the holocaust, you can ban the bomb in a feather boa just as well as without, and a mild interest in the length of hemlines doesn't necessarily disqualify you from reading Das Kapital and agreeing with every word."

Elizabeth Bibesco

Clutter

"In many ways it is easier not to have lots of things."
Brenda Blethyn
You, 7 December 2003

"I'm learning to love minimalism ... a lot of the clutter in my life was things you couldn't bear to get rid of – and you realise you don't need that stuff. It was very cleansing."

Leslie Ash
Radio Times, 6–12 December 2003

Co-dependence

"It is easier to live through someone else than to become complete in yourself."
Betty Friedan

"It's far better to be wanted than needed."
Brenda Blethyn
You, 7 December 2003

Coffee

You Know You've Had Too Much Coffee When ...

You grind your coffee beans in your mouth.

You lick your coffeepot clean.

You spend every vacation visiting "Maxwell House".

You're the employee of the month at the local coffeehouse and you don't even work there.

Your eyes stay open when you sneeze.

You're so jittery that people use your hands to blend their margaritas.

Your only source of nutrition comes from "Sweet & Low".

You go to AA meetings just for the free coffee.

You've built a miniature city out of little plastic stirrers.

People get dizzy just watching you.

Starbucks owns the mortgage on your house.

You're so wired, you pick up FM radio.

Your life's goal is to "amount to a hill of beans".

Instant coffee takes too long.

You want to be cremated just so you can spend the rest of eternity in a coffee can.

You go to sleep just so you can wake up and smell the coffee.

You name your cats "Cream" and "Sugar".

Your lips are permanently stuck in the sipping position.

You don't tan, you roast.

You introduce your spouse as your "Coffeemate".

You think CPR stands for "Coffee Provides Resuscitation".

"Behind every successful woman ... is a substantial amount of coffee."
Stephanie Piro

"Never drink black coffee at lunch; it will keep you awake all afternoon."
Jilly Cooper

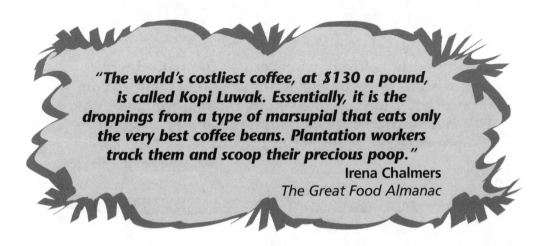

"The world's costliest coffee, at $130 a pound, is called Kopi Luwak. Essentially, it is the droppings from a type of marsupial that eats only the very best coffee beans. Plantation workers track them and scoop their precious poop."
Irena Chalmers
The Great Food Almanac

Commitment

"Let me die to myself, that so I may serve thee: let me live to thee, who in thyself art the true life."
St Teresa of Avila

"It's time for every one of us to roll up our sleeves and put ourselves at the top of the commitment list."
Marian Wright Edelman

"To believe in something yet to be proved and to underwrite it with our lives; it is the only way we can leave the future open."
Lillian Smith

"The dedicated life is the life worth living. You must give with your whole heart."
Annie Dillard

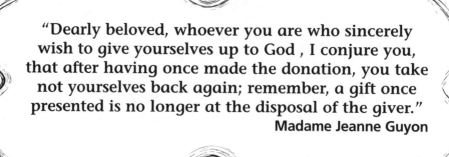

"Dearly beloved, whoever you are who sincerely wish to give yourselves up to God , I conjure you, that after having once made the donation, you take not yourselves back again; remember, a gift once presented is no longer at the disposal of the giver."
Madame Jeanne Guyon

Communication

"Let us make a special effort to stop communicating with each other, so we can have some conversation."
Judith Martin (Miss Manners)

"Make sure you have finished speaking before your audience has finished listening."
Dorothy Sarnoff

"Communication is a continual balancing act, juggling the conflicting needs for intimacy and independence."
Deborah Tannen
You Just Don't Understand

What are the three fastest means of communication?

1. Internet
2. Telephone
3. Telawoman

Compassion

"The goal of compassion is not to care because someone is like us but to care because they are themselves."

Mary Lou Randour

Competition

"Compete against yourself, not others, for that is who your best competition truly is."
Peggy Flemming

"There are two kinds of people, those who do the work and those who take the credit. Try to be in the first group; there is less competition there."

Indira Gandhi

Don't compare yourself to the best others can do, but to the best you can do.

Anon

Completion

"All respect comes from persisting to completion."

Melissa Lima

"The completion of an important project has every right to be dignified by a natural grieving process. Something that required the best of you has ended. You will miss it."

Anne Wilson Schaef

"Sometimes when you think you are done, it is just the edge of beginning. Probably that's why we decide we're done. It's getting too scary. We are touching down onto something real. It is beyond the point when you think you are done that often something strong comes out."

Natalie Goldberg

"When I stand before God at the end of my life, I would hope that I would not have a single bit of talent left, and could say, 'I used everything you gave me.'"

Erma Bombeck

Compromise

"The minute you settle for less than you deserve, you get even less than you settled for."

Maureen Dowd
New York Times

"Standing in the middle of the road is very dangerous; you get knocked down by the traffic from both sides."
Margaret Thatcher

Confidence

"I am very shy but I hide it well. It's almost like a sickness. But I had to work ... so I pushed myself, and little by little I started to cover up my shyness and pretend to be somebody else, and little by little people believed me."

Sophia Loren
Times Magazine, 21 June 2003

"I was always looking outside myself for strength and confidence, but it comes from within. It is there all the time."

Anna Freud

"Real confidence comes from knowing and accepting yourself – your strengths and your limitations – in contrast to depending on affirmation from others."
Judith M Bardwick

"Confidence is down to how you feel about yourself – it's so much easier if you are happy about your appearance."

Joyce Green
Weight Watcher's Magazine, June 2003

"We have to have faith in ourselves. I have never met a woman who, deep down in her core, really believes she has great legs. And if she suspects that she might have great legs, then she's convinced that she has a shrill voice and no neck."

Cynthia Heimel

Conformity

"Normal is not something to aspire to; it's something to get away from."
Jodie Foster

"The reward for conformity was that everyone liked you but yourself."
Rita Mae Brown
Venus Envy

Conscience

"Conscience ... is the impulse to do right because it is right, regardless of personal ends."
Margaret C Graham
"A Matter of Conscience", in
Do They Really Respect Us? and Other Essays

"Conscience that isn't hitched up to common sense is a mighty dangerous thing."
Margaret Deland
The Promises of Alice

Contentment

"In spite of illness, in spite even of the arch-enemy sorrow, one can remain alive long past the usual date of disintegration if one is unafraid of change, insatiable in intellectual curiosity, interested in big things, and happy in small ways."

Edith Wharton

"A woman's discontent increases in exact proportion to her development."
Elizabeth Cady Stanton

Conversation

"The real art of conversation is not only to say the right thing at the right place but to leave unsaid the wrong thing at the tempting moment."
Dorothy Nevill

"There is no such thing as conversation. It is an illusion. There are intersecting monologues, that is all."

Rebecca West

"Most conversations are simply monologues delivered in the presence of witnesses."
Margaret Millar

*"If you explore beneath shyness or party chit-chat,
you can sometimes turn a dull exchange into an intriguing one.
I've found this to be particularly true in the case of professors or
intellectuals, who are full of fascinating information, but need
encouragement before they'll divulge it."*

Joyce Carol Oates

**"It is not what we learn in conversation that enriches us.
It is the elation that comes of swift contact with tingling
currents of thought."**

Agnes Repplier

Cooking

*"I refuse to believe that
trading recipes is silly.
Tuna fish casserole is at
least as real as
corporate stock."*

Barbara Grizzuti Harrison

"I don't even
butter my bread. I
consider that cooking."
Katherine Cebrian

*"If a man prepares
dinner for you and the
salad contains three or
more types of lettuce, he
is serious."*
Rita Rudner

**"Remember that there
must be someone to cook
the meals, and count
yourself happy in being
able to serve like
Martha."**

St Teresa of Avila

*"I find the act of baking very calming, and there's something
so pleasurable in providing a cake for a friend."*

Nigella Lawson
Telegraph Magazine, 28 February 2004

There is one thing
more exasperating than a spouse
who can cook and won't, and that's
a spouse who can't cook and will.

Anon

"You don't have to
cook fancy or complicated
masterpieces – just good
food from fresh
ingredients."
Julia Child

Cost

*"Some prices are just too high, no matter how much you may want the prize.
The one thing you can't trade for your heart's desire is your heart."*
Lois McMaster Bujold
Memory

*"Everyone must learn this lesson somewhere – that it cost
something to be what you are."*
Shirley Abbott

"To be in the right is often an expensive business."
Phyllis Bottome
Danger Signals

*"To gain what is worth having, it may be necessary
to lose everything else."*
Bernadette Devlin

Courage

"Courage is the willingness to stay open to our fear and rawness, without running away."

Sister Stanislaus Kennedy
Gardening the Soul

"The only courage that matters is the kind that gets you from one moment to the next."

Mignon McLaughlin
The Second Neurotic's Notebook

"Courage is the price that life exacts for granting peace."

Amelia Earhart
Courage

"Courage is fear that has said its prayers."

Dorothy Bernard

"Life shrinks or expands in proportion to one's courage."

Anaïs Nin

"Courage is saying: 'Maybe what I'm doing isn't working; maybe I should try something else.'"

Anna Lappe
O Magazine, June 2003

"O merciful God, be thou now unto us a strong tower of defence, we humbly entreat thee. Give us grace to await thy leisure, and patiently to bear what thou doest to us, nothing doubting, or mistrusting thy goodness towards us; for thou knowest what is good for us better than we do."

Lady Jane Grey

"Cowards falter, but danger is often overcome by those who nobly dare."
Elizabeth, the Queen Mother

"Courage is the ladder on which all the other virtues mount."
Clare Boothe Luce

"Courage is very important. Like a muscle, it is strengthened by use."
Ruth Gordon

"Courage is more exhilarating than fear; and in the long run it is easier.
Eleanor Roosevelt

"It's better to be a lion for a day than a sheep all your life."
Sister Elizabeth Kenny

Creativity

"Many people are inventive, sometimes cleverly so. But real creativity begins with the drive to work on and on and on."
Margueritte Harmon Bro
Sarah

"Creativity comes from trust. Trust your instincts. And never hope more than you work."
Rita Mae Brown
Starting from Scratch

"Creativity is a lot like looking at the world through a kaleidoscope. You look at a set of elements, the same ones everyone else sees, but then reassemble those floating bits and pieces into an enticing new possibility."
Rosabeth Moss Kanter

"To be surrounded by beautiful things has much influence upon the human creature; to make beautiful things has more."
Charlotte Perkins Gilman

"I do believe it is possible to create, even without ever writing a word or painting a picture, by simply moulding one's inner life. And that too is a deed."
Etty Hillesum

"Creativity is ... seeing something that doesn't exist already. You need to find out how you can bring it into being and that way be a playmate with God."
Michele Shea

"When we are writing, or painting, or composing, we are, during the time of creativity, freed from normal restrictions, and are opened to a wider world, where colours are brighter, sounds clearer, and people more wondrously complex than we normally realise."
Madeleine L'Engle
Walking on Water

Criticism

"I find that the very thing that I get criticised for, which is usually being different and just doing my own thing and just being original, is the very thing that's making me successful."

Shania Twain

"Dare to risk public criticism."
Mary Kay Ash

Curiosity

"Be less curious about people and more curious about ideas."
Marie Curie

"Curiosity is one of those insatiable passions that grow by gratification."
Sarah Scott
A Description of Millennium Hall

"I think, at a child's birth, if a mother could ask a fairy godmother to endow it with the most useful gift, that gift would be curiosity."

Eleanor Roosevelt

"The curious are always in some danger."

Jeanette Winterson
Oranges Are Not the Only Fruit

Death

"People living deeply have no fear of death."

Anaïs Nin

"There is nothing like death. Everything that approaches it is metaphor."

Flora Johnson

"At the end of this life, which seems to me so near eternity, I am filled not only with happiness in all the good God is giving me, but in all that he has given me."

Mother Marie Adele Garnier

"Dying is an integral part of life ... but whereas birth is cause for celebration, death has become a dreaded and unspeakable issue to be avoided by every means possible in our modern society ... It is perhaps this inevitable and unpredictable quality that makes death so frightening to many people. Especially those who put a high value on being in control of their own existence are offended by the thought that they too are subject to the forces of death."

Elisabeth Kübler-Ross

Deception

"Deception is a cruel act … It often has many players on different stages that corrode the soul."
Donna A Favors

"It is astonishing what force, purity, and wisdom it requires for a human being to keep clear of falsehoods."
Margaret Fuller

"Some women can be fooled all of the time, and all women can be fooled some of the time, but the same woman can't be fooled by the same man in the same way more than half of the time."
Helen Rowland

"I know they are most deceived that trust most in themselves."
Queen Elizabeth I

Defeat

"We are not interested in possibilities of defeat. They do not exist."
Queen Victoria

"I just refuse to give up longer than a couple of weeks."
Cybill Shepherd

"There are many victories worse than a defeat."
George Eliot

Desire

"**The desire of the man is for the woman, but the desire of the woman is for the desire of the man.**"
Germaine Necker, Madame de Staël

"How helpless we are, like netted birds, when we are caught by desire!"
Belva Plain

Determination

"*It is worth mentioning, for future reference, that the creative power which bubbles so pleasantly in beginning a new book quiets down after a time, and one goes on more steadily. Doubts creep in. Then one becomes resigned. Determination not to give in, and the sense of an impending shape, keeps one at it more than anything.*"
Virginia Woolf

"The glass ceiling gets more pliable when you turn up the heat."
Pauline Kezer

"You may have to fight a battle more than once to win it."
Margaret Thatcher

"*We can do anything we want to do if we stick to it long enough.*"
Helen Keller

"Getting ahead in a difficult profession requires avid faith in yourself. That is why some people with mediocre talent, but with great inner drive, go much further than people with vastly superior talent."

Sophia Loren

Diet

"We are indeed much more than what we eat, but what we eat can nevertheless help us to be much more than what we are."

Adele Davis

The second day of a diet is always easier than the first. By the second day you're off it.

The older you get, the tougher it is to lose weight, because by then your body and your fat are really good friends.

Anon

"Nobody's last words have ever been, 'I wish I'd eaten more rice cakes.'"

Amy Krouse Rosenthal

The "Good Intentions" Diet:

Breakfast:
> Half a grapefruit
> 1 slice whole wheat toast
> 8 ounces skimmed milk

Lunch:
> 4 ounces lean steamed chicken breast
> 1 cup steamed spinach
> 1 cup herb tea
> 1 chocolate digestive

Mid–afternoon snack:
> The rest of chocolate digestives in the packet
> 2 pints ice cream, nuts, cherries and whipped cream
> 1 jar hot fudge sauce

Dinner:
> 2 loaves garlic bread
> 4 cans or 1 large bottle of cola
> 1 large sausage, mushroom and cheese pizza
> 3 chocolate peanut bars

Late evening news:
> Entire frozen cheesecake (eaten directly from freezer)

HOW TO WEIGH YOURSELF!

1. Weigh yourself with clothes on, after dinner … as well as in the morning, without clothes, before breakfast, because it's nice to see how much weight you've lost overnight.
2. Never weigh yourself with wet hair.
3. When weighing, remove everything, including glasses. In this case, blurred vision is an asset. Don't forget the earrings; these things can weigh at least a pound.
4. Use cheap scales only, never the medical kind, because the cheap ones are always five pounds off … to your advantage.
5. Always go to the bathroom first.
6. Stand with arms raised, making pressure on the scale lighter.
7. Don't eat or drink in the morning until AFTER you've weighed in, completely naked, of course.
8. Weigh yourself after a haircut; this is good for at least half a pound of hair (hopefully).
9. Exhale with all your might BEFORE stepping onto the scale (air has to weigh something, right?).
10. Start out with just one foot on the scale, then holding onto the towel rack in front of you, slowly edge your other foot on and slowly let go of the rack. Admittedly, this takes time, but it's worth it. You will weigh at least two pounds less than if you'd stepped on normally.

Diet Tip

Restaurants will almost always throw you out before you can eat too much.

Difference

"There is more difference within the sexes than between them."
Ivy Compton-Burnett
Mother and Son

"We should acknowledge differences; we should greet differences, until difference makes no difference any more."
Dr Adela Allen

"The real difference between men and women is that while men fear pity, women fear envy. Thus men like to see themselves, and be seen, as happier than they might feel, women unhappier than they might be perceived."

Nigella Lawson
Daily Telegraph

Different

"Don't dare to be different, dare to be yourself – if that doesn't make you different then something is wrong."
Laura Baker

"In order to be irreplaceable one must always be different."
Coco Chanel

"We all live with the objective of being happy; our lives are all different and yet the same."
Anne Frank

"What is right for one soul may not be right for another. It may mean having to stand on your own and do something strange in the eyes of others."
Eileen Caddy

Difficulty

"The most difficult thing is the decision to act; the rest is merely tenacity. The fears are paper tigers. You can do anything you decide to do. You can act to change and control your life; and the procedure, the process, is its own reward."
Amelia Earhart

"There are two ways of meeting difficulties: you alter the difficulties or you alter yourself to meet them."
Phyllis Bottome

"In every crisis there is a message. Crises are nature's way of forcing change – breaking down old structures, shaking loose negative habits so that something new and better can take their place."
Susan L Taylor

"Everybody has difficult years, but a lot of times the difficult years end up being the greatest years of your whole entire life, if you survive them."
Brittany Murphy
Seventeen Magazine, September 2003

"God wants to use the difficulties in your life not to punish or to hurt you but to draw you to himself."
Nancy Guthrie
Holding on to Hope

"We know that God gives us every grace, every abundant grace; and although we are so weak of ourselves, this grace is able to carry us through every obstacle and difficulty."
Elizabeth Ann Seton

Direction

"I see my path, but I don't know where it leads. Not knowing where I'm going is what inspires me to travel it."
Rosalia de Castro

"When you are on the right path, the doors open ... "
Kathleen Griffin
Church Times,
24 October 2003

"It is good to have an end to journey towards; but it is the journey that matters in the end."
Ursula K LeGuin

"Of any stopping place in life, it is good to ask whether it will be a good place from which to go on as well as a good place to remain."
Mary Catherine Bateson

"Don't spend time beating on a wall hoping to transform it into a door."
Dr Laura Schlessinger

"If you stop searching, you stop living, because then you're dwelling in the past. If you're not reaching forward to any growth or future, you might as well be dead."
Wynn Bulock

"When you come to a roadblock, take a detour."
Mary Kay Ash

"It is important that we know how to read our own history, to see the turning points, the moments of change, the unfolding of God's plan for us at each new step of the way."
Esther de Waal
Seeking God: The Way of St Benedict

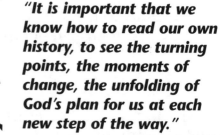

"Some lives drift here and there like reeds in a stream, depending on changing currents for their activity. Others are like swimmers knowing the depth of the water. Each stroke helps them onward to a definite objective."

Margaret Sanger

Discipline

"Without discipline, there's no life at all."
Katharine Hepburn

"Some people regard discipline as a chore. For me, it is a kind of order that sets me free to fly."
Julie Andrews

Discretion

"The sweat of hard work is not to be displayed. It is much more graceful to appear favoured by the gods."
Maxine Hong Kingston
The Woman Warrior

"It is far more impressive when others discover your good qualities without your help."
Judith S Martin

"Never complain. Never explain."
Katharine Hepburn

Divorce

"I had no idea emotional pain could be so intense, just so utterly painful. It is hard to explain. I think because the wounds are invisible people think they are not there."
Jennifer Croly
Missing being Mrs

Doubt

"Doubt whom you will, but never yourself."
Christine Bovee

"The minute one utters a certainty, the opposite comes to mind."
May Sarton
Mrs Stevens Hears the Mermaids Singing

Dreams

"I've dreamt in my life dreams that have stayed with me ever after, and changed my ideas; they've gone through and through me, like wine through water, and altered the colour of my mind."

Emily Brontë

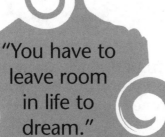

"You have to leave room in life to dream."
Buffy Sainte-Marie

"Dreams come in a size too big so that we may grow into them."
Josie Bissett

"Women have to summon up courage to fulfil dormant dreams."
Alice Walker

"If we have not achieved our early dreams, we must either find new ones or see what we can salvage from the old. If we have accomplished what we set out to do in our youth, we need not weep like Alexander the Great that we have no more worlds to conquer."
Rosalynn Carter

> *"There are people who put their dreams in a little box and say, 'Yes, I've got dreams, of course I've got dreams.' Then they put the box away and bring it out once in awhile to look in it, and yep, they're still there. These are great dreams, but they never even get out of the box. It takes an uncommon amount of guts to put your dreams on the line, to hold them up and say, 'How good or how bad am I?' That's where courage comes in."*
>
> **Erma Bombeck**

"Our life is composed greatly from dreams, from the unconscious, and they must be brought into connection with action. They must be woven together."

Anaïs Nin

"We don't have an eternity to realise our dreams, only the time we are here."

Susan Taylor

"The thing you have to be prepared for is that other people don't always dream your dream."

Linda Ronstadt

"The future belongs to those who believe in the beauty of their dreams."

Eleanor Roosevelt

Driving

Two cars are waiting behind one another at a stoplight. The light turns green, but the man in the front car doesn't notice it. A woman in the car behind him watches the traffic pass around them. She begins pounding on her steering wheel and yelling at the man to move. He doesn't move.

The woman is going ballistic inside her car, ranting and raving at the man, pounding on her steering wheel and dashboard. The light turns yellow. The woman begins to blow the car horn, and scream curses at the man.

The driver in the lead car, hearing the commotion, looks up, sees the yellow light and accelerates through the intersection just as the light turns red.

The woman is beside herself, screaming in frustration as she misses her chance to get through the intersection. As she is still in mid-rant she hears a tap on her window and looks up into the barrel of a gun held by a very serious-looking policeman.

The policeman tells her to shut off her car while keeping both hands in sight. She complies, speechless at what is happening. After she shuts off the engine, the policeman orders her to exit her car with her hands up. She gets out and he orders her to turn and place her hands on her car. She turns, places her hands on the car roof and is quickly cuffed and hustled into the patrol car. She is too bewildered by the chain of events to ask any questions and is driven in silence to the police station where she is fingerprinted, photographed, searched, booked and placed in a cell.

After a couple of hours, a policeman approaches the cell and opens the door for her. She is escorted back to the booking desk where the original officer is waiting with her personal effects.

He hands her the bag containing her things, and says, "I'm really sorry for this mistake. But you see, I pulled up behind your car while you were blowing your horn and cursing at the car in front of you. Then I noticed the "Choose GOD" licence-plate holder, the "What Would Jesus Do?" and "Follow Me to Sunday School" bumper stickers, and the chrome-plated Christian fish emblem on the trunk, so naturally I assumed you had stolen the car."

Remember ... when everything's coming your way, you're in the wrong lane.

Did you hear about the woman who was pulled over for speeding? The policeman got out of his car and the woman rolled down her window.

"I've been waiting for you all day," the policeman said.

The woman replied, "Well, I got here as fast as I could!"

You know, somebody actually complimented me on my driving today. They left a little note on the windscreen. It said: "Parking Fine."

That was so nice.

She who hesitates is not only lost, but miles from the next exit.

Anon

Drive carefully.
It's not only cars
that can be recalled
by their maker.

Duty

"Conscientious people are apt to see their duty in that which is the most painful course."

George Eliot
The Mill on the Floss

"People tend to forget their duties but remember their rights."
Indira Gandhi
Last Words

"The children will not leave unless I do. I shall not leave unless their father does, and the king will not leave the country in any circumstances whatever."
Elizabeth, the Queen Mother
(in response to the bombing of Buckingham Palace during WWII)

"The first duty of a human being is to assume the right relationship to society – more briefly, to find your real job, and do it."
Charlotte Perkins Gilman

Education

"**People commonly educate their children as they build their houses, according to some plan they think beautiful, without considering whether it is suited to the purposes for which they are designed.**"
Mary Wortley Montagu

"Real education should educate us out of self into something far finer: into a selflessness which links us with all humanity."
Lady Nancy Astor

"*Education is the mental railway, beginning at birth and running on to eternity. No hand can lay it in the right direction but the hand of a mother.*"
Mrs H O Ward

"It has always seemed strange to me that in our endless discussions about education so little stress is laid on the pleasure of becoming an educated person, the enormous interest it adds to life. To be able to be caught up into the world of thought – that is to be educated."

Edith Hamilton

"It is as impossible to withhold education from the receptive mind, as it is impossible to force it upon the unreasoning."
Agnes Repplier

Elegance

"*Elegance is not the prerogative of those who have just escaped from adolescence, but of those who have already taken possession of their future.*"

"Elegance does not consist in putting on a new dress."

"Elegance is refusal."

Coco Chanel

Encouragement

"Those who are lifting the world upward and onward are those who encourage more than criticise."

Elizabeth Harrison

"We live by encouragement and die without it – slowly, sadly, angrily."
Celeste Holm

Enthusiasm

"Enthusiasm is contagious. Be a carrier."
Susan Rabin
How to Attract Anyone, Anytime, Anyplace

"Enthusiasm is a divine possession."

Margaret Sanger

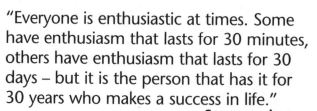

"Everyone is enthusiastic at times. Some have enthusiasm that lasts for 30 minutes, others have enthusiasm that lasts for 30 days – but it is the person that has it for 30 years who makes a success in life."
Source unknown

Environment

"A society in which consumption has to be artificially stimulated in order to keep production going is a society founded on trash and waste, and such a society is a house built on sand."
Dorothy L Sayers

"We do not inherit the land; we borrow it from our children."
Native American saying

"Future generations are unlikely to condone our lack of prudent concern for the integrity of the natural world that supports all life."
Rachel Carson
Silent Spring

Equality

"We have to be careful in this era of radical feminism, not to emphasise an equality of the sexes that leads women to imitate men to prove their equality. To be equal does not mean you have to be the same."

Eva Burrows

"One of the things about equality is not just that you be treated equally to a man, but that you treat yourself equally to the way you treat a man."
Marlo Thomas

"The demand for equal rights in every vocation of life is just and fair; but, after all, the most vital right is the right to love and be loved."
Emma Goldman

We will not have true equality until there are mediocre women in the top jobs.
Anon, courtesy of Dr Louise Baron

"Equality … is the result of human organisation. We are not born equal."
Hannah Arendt

Escape

"The idea of escaping to somewhere else appeals to women because our lives are one big juggling act."

Lindsay Duncan
Good Housekeeping, April 2004

Evil

"Evil
is not something
superhuman; it's something
less than human."
Agatha Christie
The Pale Horse

"Evil is obvious only in retrospect."
Gloria Steinem
Outrageous Acts and Everyday Rebellions

Excellence

Excellence can be attained …
if you care more than others think is wise,
risk more than others think is safe,
dream more than others think is practical,
and expect more than others think is possible.
Source unknown

"I strive for excellence. Nothing is perfect, but if it gets to a certain level, it's pretty good and that's all you can do."
Barbra Streisand
Reader's Digest, November 2003

"Be a first-rate version of yourself, not a second-rate version of someone else."
Judy Garland

"There is nothing immoral or selfish about having high standards."
Cheryl Richardson

"We only do well the things we like doing."
Colette
Prisons and Paradise

"The secret of joy in work is contained in one word – excellence. To know how to do something well is to enjoy it."
Pearl S Buck
The Joy of Children

"Quality is never an accident. It is always the result of high intention, sincere effort, intelligent direction, and skilful execution. It represents the wise choice of many alternatives."
Willa A Foster
Bits & Pieces

Expectations

Expect the people you love to be better. It helps them to become better. But don't get upset when they fail. It helps them keep trying.

Anon

"A master can tell you what he expects of you. A teacher, though, awakens your own expectations."

Patricia Neal

"Who is ever adequate? We all create situations each other can't live up to, then break our hearts at them because they don't."

Elizabeth Bowen

Experience

"You gain strength, courage, and confidence by every experience by which you really stop to look fear in the face. You are able to say to yourself, 'I lived through this horror. I can take the next thing that comes along.'"

Eleanor Roosevelt

"Experiencing life through a book can help you learn without all the pain of going through the experiences first-hand."

Bette Greene

"We are volcanoes. When we women offer our experience as our truth, as human truth, all the maps change. There are new mountains."

Ursula K LeGuin

Failure

"For every failure, there's an alternative course of action. You just have to find it."
Mary Kay Ash

"Do not allow yourself to be disheartened by any failure as long as you do your best."
Mother Teresa

"The person interested in success has to learn to view failure as a healthy, inevitable part of the process of getting to the top."
Dr Joyce Brothers

"When we can begin to take our failures non-seriously, it means we are ceasing to be afraid of them."
Katherine Mansfield

"Three failures denote uncommon strength. A weakling has not enough grit to fail thrice."
Minna Thomas Antrim

"Failure after long perseverance is much grander than never to have a striving good enough to be called a failure."
George Eliot

Faith

"For those who believe, no explanation is necessary. For those who do not believe, no explanation is possible."

Anon

"Faith is the strength by which a shattered world shall emerge into the light."
Helen Keller

"Seeds of faith are always within us; sometimes it takes a crisis to nourish and encourage their growth."
Susan L Taylor

"Trusting God when the miracle does not come, when the urgent prayers get no answer, when there is only darkness – this is the kind of faith God values perhaps most of all."
Nancy Guthrie
Holding on to Hope

"If faith is lacking, it is because there is too much selfishness, too much concern for personal gain. For faith to be true, it has to be generous and loving. Love and faith go together; they complete each other."
Mother Teresa

"First we have to believe, and then we believe."
Martha Graham

Family

"The only perfect love to be found on earth is …
the wordless commitment of families, which takes
as its model mother-love."

Germaine Greer

"Nobody,
who has not
been in the
interior of a family,
can say what the
difficulties of any
individual of that family
may be."

Jane Austen

"Family faces are magic mirrors.
Looking at people who belong to
us, we see the past, present,
and future."

Gail Lumet Buckley

"The family is changing not
disappearing. We have to broaden our
understanding of it, look for the new
metaphors."

Mary Catherine Bateson

"Those who think the
family has had its
day should think
again."

Eva Burrows

"Real families are not made simply by
giving birth … families are made
through love and commitment, through
unselfish caring for others' needs."

Beth Spring
Childless: The Hurt and the Hope

"If it is working well, [the family] gives you the security, love and confidence that nothing else will provide."
Esther Rantzen
The Times, 15 July 2003

"To us, family means putting your arms around each other and being there."
Barbara Bush

"*In some families, please is described as the magic word. In our house, however, it was sorry.*"
Margaret Laurence

"*When you look at your life, the greatest happinesses are family happinesses.*"
Dr Joyce Brothers

"The informality of family life is a blessed condition that allows us to become our best while looking our worst."
Marge Kennedy

"*The great advantage of living in a large family is that early lesson of life's essential unfairness.*"
Nancy Mitford

"No matter how many communes anybody invents, the family always creeps back."
Margaret Mead

Fashion

"Fashion is made to become unfashionable."
Coco Chanel

"Fashion is architecture: it is a matter of proportions."
Coco Chanel

"Forty-somethings can get away with all sorts of looks designed for younger women, provided they are the right ones."

Sophie Laybourne
Telegraph Weekend, 21 June 2003

"Women dress alike all over the world: they dress to be annoying to other women."

Elsa Schiaparelli

"Fashion is not something that exists in dresses only. Fashion is in the sky, in the street; fashion has to do with ideas, the way we live, what is happening."

Coco Chanel

"Oh, never mind the fashion. When one has a style of one's own, it is twenty times better."

Margaret Olifant

Fate

"Events that are predestined require but little management. They manage themselves. They slip into place while we sleep, and suddenly we are aware that the thing we fear to attempt is already accomplished."
Amelia Barr

"Believing in fate produces fate. Believing in freedom will create infinite possibilities."
Ayn Rand

Father

"Fathers represent another way of looking at life – the possibility of an alternative dialogue."
Louise J Kaplan
Oneness and Separateness: From Infant to Individual

Fear

"A fool without fear is sometimes wiser than an angel with fear."

Lady Nancy Astor
My Two Countries

"Don't be afraid if things seem difficult in the beginning. That's only the initial impression. The important thing is not to retreat; you have to master yourself."

Olga Korbut

"Fear is possibly a woman's greatest weapon against herself and until it's overcome, there's no moving on."

Erica James
Woman & Home, October 2003

"Fear not those who argue but those who dodge."
Marie von Ebner-Eschenbach
Aphorisms

"Our deepest fear is not that we are inadequate. Our deepest fear is that we are powerful beyond measure. It is our Light, not our Darkness, that most frightens us."
Marianne Williamson

"There are four ways you can handle fear. You can go over it, under it, or around it. But if you are ever to put fear behind you, you must walk straight through it. Once you put fear behind you, leave it there."

Donna A Favors

"Our fears are a treasure house of self-knowledge if we explore them."
Marilyn Ferguson

"For the most part, fear is nothing but an illusion. When you share it with someone else, it tends to disappear."

Marilyn C Barrick

"I think what weakens people most is fear of wasting their strength."
Etty Hillesum
An Interrupted Life

"I will not live an unlived life. I will not live in fear of falling or catching fire."
Dawna Markova

"The moment we begin to fear the opinions of others and hesitate to tell the truth that is in us, and from motives of policy are silent when we should speak, the divine floods of light and life no longer flow into our souls."
Elizabeth Cady Stanton

Feelings

"I think one's feelings waste themselves in words; they ought all to be distilled into actions which bring results."
Florence Nightingale

"Our feelings are our most genuine paths to knowledge."
Audre Lord

Feminism

"The people I'm furious with are the women's liberationists. They keep getting up on soapboxes and proclaiming women are brighter than men. That's true, but it should be kept quiet or it ruins the whole racket."

Anita Loos
New York Times, 10 February 1974

 "Feminism directly confronts the idea that one person or set of people [has] the right to impose definitions of reality on others."
Liz Stanley and Sue Wise

"Feminism and Christianity have not travelled well together. Polarised perception – acute political correctness versus staunch patriarchy – has not helped either cause … Christian feminist theology would best serve the Church by continuing to appreciate the male."

Claire Shelley
Church of England Newspaper, 18 September 2003

"My idea of feminism is self-determination, and it's very open-ended: every woman has the right to become herself, and do whatever she needs to do."
Ani DiFranco

"Feminism is the radical notion that women are people."
Cheris Kramarae and Paula Treichler

"You don't have to be anti-man to be pro-woman."
Jane Galvin Lewis

Food

"One can not think well, love well, sleep well, if one has not dined well."
Virginia Woolf
A Room of One's Own

"Nothing stimulates the practised cook's imagination like an egg."
Irma Rombauer

"Eat breakfast like a king, lunch like a prince, and dinner like a pauper."
Adele Davis

"One can say everything best over a meal."
George Eliot

"Food is the most primitive form of comfort."
Sheila Graham

"I am not a glutton – I am an explorer of food."
Erma Bombeck

"Glutton: one who digs her grave with her teeth."
French proverb

"Tomatoes and oregano make it Italian; wine and tarragon make it French. Sour cream makes it Russian; lemon and cinnamon make it Greek. Soy sauce makes it Chinese; garlic makes it good."
Alice May Brock

Foolishness

"A fool is someone whose pencil wears out before its eraser does."
Marilyn vos Savant

"It's better to be thought of as a fool and to surprise people once in a while than to be thought of as a brain and to let people down when they need you the most."
Julie Melenson

"Illusion is the dust the devil throws in the eyes of the foolish."
Minna Antrim
Naked Truth and Veiled Allusions

Take your time and see if you can read each line aloud without a mistake:

This is this cat
This is is cat
This is how cat
This is to cat
This is keep cat
This is a cat
This is fool cat
This is busy cat
This is for cat
This is forty cat
This is seconds cat

Now go back and read the THIRD word in each line from the top down …

She who knows not and knows not that she knows not is a fool – avoid her!
She who knows and knows not that she knows is asleep – waken her!
But she who knows and knows that she knows is a wise woman – know her.
Proverb

Forgiveness

"Nothing brings families together faster than forgiveness."
Dr Joyce Brothers
"Reconnect with your family", *Parade Magazine*, 11 April 2001

"Forgiveness was not a word I used at first but, hearing the bitterness and anger, I knew I didn't want to go down that road. So I prayed to be able to forgive."
Denise Green
Telegraph Magazine, 20 December 2003

"It is easy to forgive others their mistakes; it takes more grit to forgive them for having witnessed your own."
Jessamyn West

"Forgiving does not mean forgetting …
We need to forgive – and to remember, so that the same things don't happen to us again."
Kathleen Griffin
"How do you truly forgive?", *Church Times*, 24 October 2003

"Where there is guilt and remorse, forgiveness is the beginning of healing. And where there is forgiveness, there is life and hope and love."
Elaine Storkey
Losing a Child

"Forgiveness is a virtue of the brave."
Indira Gandhi

"Forgiveness is the key to action and freedom."
Hannah Arendt

"Forgiveness is the key that unlocks the door of resentment and the handcuffs of hate. It is a power that breaks the chains of bitterness and the shackles of selfishness. He who cannot forgive others breaks the bridge over which he himself must pass."
Corrie ten Boom

"Holding on to anger, resentment and hurt only gives you tense muscles, a headache and a sore jaw from clenching your teeth. Forgiveness gives you back the laughter and the lightness in your life."
Joan Lunden
Healthy Living Magazine

It isn't always enough to be forgiven by others. Sometimes you have to learn to forgive yourself.
Anon

Freedom

"Intellectual freedom depends upon material things. Poetry depends upon intellectual freedom. And women have always been poor, not for two hundred years merely, but from the beginning of time."
Virginia Woolf
A Room of One's Own

"A life of reaction is a life of slavery, intellectually and spiritually. One must fight for a life of action, not reaction."
Rita Mae Brown

"Who knows what women can be when they are finally free to be themselves."
Betty Friedan

"Self-reliance is the only road to true freedom, and being one's own person is its ultimate reward."
Patricia Sampson

"Freedom means choosing your burden."
Hephzibah Menuhin

"Freedom is always and exclusively freedom for the one who thinks differently."
Rosa Luxemburg

 "I was determined to achieve the total freedom that our history lessons taught us we were entitled to, no matter what the sacrifice."
Rosabeth Moss Kanter

Friend

"**A true friend is someone who reaches for your hand and touches your heart.**"

Heather Pryor

A friend is someone who knows the song in your heart, and can sing it back to you when you have forgotten the words.

Anon

"True friends are those who really know you but love you anyway."

Edna Buchanan

"Sometimes being a friend means mastering the art of timing. There is a time for silence. A time to let go ... And a time to prepare to pick up the pieces when it's all over."

Gloria Naylor

"I am treating you as my friend, asking you to share my present minuses in the hope that I can ask you to share my future pluses."

Katherine Mansfield

"If you have a good friend, you don't need a mirror."

Bente Borsum

Friend **115**

"It's the friends you can call up at 4 a.m. that matter."
Marlene Dietrich

"Some people go to priests; others to poetry; I to my friends."
Virginia Woolf

Friendship

"Friendship is the finest balm for the pangs of despised love."

Jane Austen

"If you make it plain you like people, it's hard for them to resist liking you back."
Lois McMaster Bujold
Diplomatic Immunity

"A friendship can weather most things and thrive in thin soil – but it needs a little mulch of letters and phone calls and small silly presents every so often – just to save it from drying out completely."
Pam Brown

"Friendship with oneself is all-important because without it one cannot be friends with anybody else in the world."
Eleanor Roosevelt

"We should not let grass grow on the path of friendship."
Marie Therese Rodet Geoffrin

*"Never refuse any advance of friendship,
for if nine out of ten bring you nothing,
one alone may repay you."*
Madame de Tencin

Future

"We may have lost the fear of the bomb in this post cold-war era, but many have not lost the fear of what the future will hold. As someone said to me recently, 'The future isn't what it used to be.'"

Eva Burrows

"Nothing is forever, and you can't plan the future."

Nina Bawden
Saga, August 2003

"What will befall us today, O God, we know not; we only know that nothing will happen which thou has not foreseen, determined, desired and ordered – that is enough for us."

Princess Elizabeth of France

"The future depends entirely on what each of us does every day."
Gloria Steinem

"I have learned to live each day as it comes, and not to borrow trouble by dreading tomorrow. It is the dark menace of the future that makes cowards of us all."

Dorothy Dix

Gardening

"Gardening is about enjoying the smell of things growing in the soil, getting dirty without feeling guilty, and generally taking the time to soak up a little peace and serenity."

Lindley Karstens
www.noproblemgarden.com

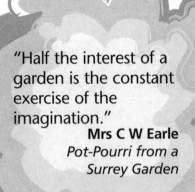

"Half the interest of a garden is the constant exercise of the imagination."
Mrs C W Earle
Pot-Pourri from a Surrey Garden

"There can be no other occupation like gardening in which, if you were to creep up behind someone at their work, you would find them smiling."
Mirabel Osler

"Gardening gives one back a sense of proportion about everything – except itself."
May Sarton
Plant Dreaming Deep

"Weather means more when you have a garden. There's nothing like listening to a shower and thinking how it is soaking in around your green beans."
Marcelene Cox

"Working in the garden ... gives me a profound feeling of inner peace."
Ruth Stout

Generosity

"That's what I consider true generosity. You give your all, and yet you always feel as if it costs you nothing."
Simone de Beauvoir

"Generosity with strings is not generosity; it is a deal."
Marya Mannes

"We are rich only through what we give, and poor only through what we refuse."
Anne-Sophie Swetchine

Genius

"What is genius, anyway, if it isn't the ability to give an adequate response to a great challenge?"
Bette Greene

"It takes people a long time to learn the difference between talent and genius, especially ambitious young men and women."
Louisa May Alcott

"Genius hath electric power which earth can never tame."
Lydia M Child

"What is genius – but the power of expressing a new individuality."
Elizabeth Barret Browning

"It takes a lot of time to be a genius; you have to sit around so much doing nothing, really doing nothing."
Gertrude Stein

Gentleness

"Practising gentleness does not mean always liking what we see or simply tolerating whatever goes on in our relationships."
Sister Stanislaus Kennedy
Gardening the Soul

"Be gentle to all, and stern with yourself."
St Teresa of Avila

Gift

"God's gifts put man's best dreams to shame."
Elizabeth Barrett Browning

"A gift – be it a present, a kind word or a job done with care and love – explains itself!"
Alice Childress

"The greatest gift is a passion for reading. It is cheap, it consoles, it distracts, it excites, it gives you knowledge of the world and experience of a wide kind. It is a moral illumination."
Elizabeth Hardwick

Giving

"Giving opens the
way for receiving."
Florence Scovel Shinn

"Giving is a necessity
sometimes ... more urgent,
indeed, than having."
Margaret Lee Runbeck

"Blessed are those who can give
without remembering, and take
without forgetting."
Princess Elizabeth Asquith Bibesco

"Some people give time, some
money, some their skills and
connections, some literally give
their life's blood. But everyone
has something to give."
Barbara Bush

"To give without any
reward, or any
notice, has a special
quality of its own."
Anne Morrow Lindbergh

Goals

B efore you begin a thing, remind yourself that
difficulties and delays quite impossible to foresee are
ahead. If you could see them clearly, naturally you
could do a great deal to get rid of them but you can't. You
can only see one thing clearly and that is your goal. Form a
mental vision of that and cling to it through thick and thin.
Words of wisdom from a woman – source unknown

"If we make our goal to
live a life of compassion
and unconditional love,
then the world will
indeed become a garden
where all kinds of flowers
can bloom and grow."
Elisabeth Kübler-Ross

"Goals too clearly
defined can
become blinkers."
Mary Catherine Bateson
Composing a Life

God

*"It seems you are so in love with your creatures that you could not
live without us! Yet you are our God, and have no need of us."*
St Catherine of Siena

"It is the creative potential itself in human beings
that is the image of God."

Mary Daly

"They say that God is everywhere,
and yet we always think of Him as somewhat of a recluse."
Emily Dickinson

*"Whatever God's dream about man may be,
it seems certain it cannot come true unless man cooperates."*
Stella Terrill Mann

*"To discover the heart of God, we need only to look up
from our circumstances and look to the Cross."*

Nancy Guthrie
Holding on to Hope

Gratitude

"Gratitude helps you to grow and expand; gratitude brings joy and laughter into your life and into the lives of all those around you."

Eileen Caddy

"There shall be eternal summer in the grateful heart."

Celia Thaxter

"*Gratitude makes sense of our past, brings peace for today, and creates a vision for tomorrow.*"

Melody Beattie

"When we choose not to focus on what is missing from our lives but are grateful for the abundance that's present – love, health, family, friends, work, the joys of nature, and personal pursuits that bring us pleasure – the wasteland of illusion falls away and we experience heaven on earth."

Sarah Ban Brethnach

Growing Up

WHEN I GROW UP

The teacher asked her class what each child wanted to become when they grew up. A chorus of responses came from all over the room.

"A football player."

"A doctor."

"An astronaut."

"The prime minister."

"A fireman."

"A teacher."

"A racing car driver."

Everyone spoke up, except Stacia.

The teacher noticed she was sitting there quiet and still. So she said to her, "Stacia, what do you want to be when you grow up?"

"Possible," Stacia replied.

"Possible?" asked the teacher.

"Yes," Stacia said. "My mum is always telling me I'm impossible. So when I grow up, I want to be possible."

"I was wise enough to never grow up while fooling most people into believing I had."
Margaret Mead

"Adults are always asking kids what they want to be when they grow up because they are looking for ideas."
Paula Poundstone

"To do life right, you have to feel like you're growing up until the day you die."
Jane Fonda

"When we were children, we used to think that when we were grown-up we would no longer be vulnerable. But to grow up is to accept vulnerability ... To be alive is to be vulnerable."
Madeleine L'Engle
Walking on Water

"You grow up the day you have your first real laugh ... at yourself."
Ethel Barrymore

Growth

"The strongest principle of growth lies in human choice."
George Eliot
Daniel Deronda

"You will not grow if you sit in a beautiful flower garden, but you will grow if you are sick, if you are in pain, if you experience losses, and if you do not put your head in the sand, but take the pain and learn to accept it, not as a curse or punishment but as a gift to you with a very, very specific purpose."
Elisabeth Kübler-Ross

"Any human anywhere will blossom in a hundred unexpected talents and capacities simply by being given the opportunity to do so."
Doris Lessing

"Each of us is many women, and each stage of life offers the potential for discovering new freedom, new growth, and new pleasures."
Penelope Washbourn

"To grow is sometimes to hurt; but who would return to smallness?"
Sarah Patton Boyle

"Growth itself contains the germ of happiness."
Pearl S Buck

"Self-development is a higher duty than self-sacrifice."
Elizabeth Cady Stanton

"You've got to continue to grow, or you're just like last night's corn bread – stale and dry."
Loretta Lynn

"It is never too late to become what you might have been."
George Eliot

"How we grow depends on how we receive what comes to us."
Sister Stanislaus Kennedy
Gardening the Soul

"We learn and grow and are transformed not so much by what we do, but by why and how we do it."
Sharon Salzberg
"The Power of Intention",
O Magazine, January 2004

"If you play it safe in life, you've decided that you don't want to grow any more."
Shirley Hufsteddler

"We do not grow absolutely, chronologically. We grow sometimes in one dimension, and not in another."
Anaïs Nin

Guidance

"It is only by following your deepest instinct that you can lead a rich life, and if you let your fear of consequence prevent you from following your deepest instinct, then your life will be safe, expedient and thin."
Katharine Butler Hathaway

"We have all a better guide in ourselves, if we would attend to it, than any other person can be."
Jane Austen
Mansfield Park

"We cannot direct the wind, but we can adjust the sails."
Bertha Calloway

"I really feel like life will dictate itself. You should allow it to unfold as naturally as possible."
Shania Twain

Habits

Bad habits are like a comfortable bed: easy to get into, but hard to get out of.

Anon

"Mindless habitual behaviour is the enemy of innovation."

Rosabeth Moss Kanter

"It's become a habit for people to blame their upbringing for everything."

Nina Bawden
Saga, August 2003

"Habits ... the only reason they persist is that they are offering some satisfaction ... You allow them to persist by not seeking any other, better form of satisfying the same needs."

Juliene Berk

Good habits result from resisting temptation.

Ancient proverb

"Curious things, habits. People themselves never knew they had them."
Agatha Christie

Watch your thoughts, they become your words,
Watch your words, they become your actions,
Watch your actions, they become your habits,
Watch your habits, they become your character,
Watch your character, it becomes your destiny.

Anon

Happiness

*"It is not easy to find happiness in ourselves,
and it is not possible to find it elsewhere."*

Agnes Repplier

"When we show concern for the happiness in others,
we ultimately enhance the happiness in ourselves."

Donna A Favors

*Happiness is like a butterfly. The more you chase it,
the more it eludes you. But if you turn your attention to other
things, it comes and sits softly on your shoulder.*

Anon

"It is only possible to live happily ever after on
a day-to-day basis."

Margaret Bonnano

"One of the keys to happiness is a bad memory."

Rita Mae Brown

"The only truly happy people are children and the creative minority."

Jean Caldwell

"It is a shock to discover that no one can expect serene and perfect happiness for always."
Elizabeth Buchan
The Good Wife

"One has a profound, if irrational, instinct in favour of the theory that the union of man and woman makes for the greatest satisfaction, the most complete happiness."
Virginia Woolf
A Room of One's Own

"Too many wish to be happy before becoming wise."
Susanne Curchod Necker

"Happiness is not a station to arrive at, but a manner of travelling."
Margaret Lee Runbeck

"If only we'd stop trying to be happy, we could have a pretty good time."
Edith Wharton

"The happiest people I have known have been those who gave themselves no concern about their own souls, but did their uttermost to mitigate the miseries of others."
Elizabeth Cady Stanton

"Happiness consists not in having much, but in being content with little."
Marguerite Gardiner

"Happiness, I do not know where to turn to discover you on earth, in the air or the sky; yet I know you exist and are no futile dream."
Rosalia de Castro

Hate

"You can envy another woman's beauty or her mind, but you only truly hate her if her house is clean and shining."

Elizabeth Buchan
The Good Wife

"In hatred as in love, we grow like the thing we brood upon. What we loathe, we graft into our very soul."

Mary Renault

Health

"Health is not simply the absence of sickness."

Hannah Green

"Health – what my friends are always drinking to before they fall down."

Phyllis Diller

"As I see it, every day you do one of two things: build health or produce disease in yourself."

Adele Davis

"It's no longer a question of staying healthy. It's a question of finding a sickness you like."

Jackie Mason

"Our health is a voyage and every illness is an adventure story."

Margiad Evans

Heartbreak

"Tears may be dried up, but the heart – never."
Marguerite de Valois

"There are many ways of breaking a heart. Stories were full of hearts being broken by love, but what really broke a heart was taking away its dream – whatever that dream might be."
Pearl S Buck

"To wear your heart on your sleeve isn't a very good plan; you should wear it inside, where it functions best."
Margaret Thatcher
Interview with Barbara Walters on ABC TV, 18 March 1987

"Beauty, more than bitterness, makes the heart break."
Sara Teasdale

Help

"Never help a child with a task at which he feels he can succeed."
Maria Montessori

"In helping others,
we shall help ourselves,
for whatever good we give
out completes the circle and
comes back to us."
Flora Edwards

"Allow yourself to
need help, to need
love, to need other
people ... now allow
yourself to receive
what is offered."
Rachel Snyder

"We can't help everyone,
but everyone can help
someone."
Dr Loretta Scott

Home

Home is the place where we grumble the most, but are often treated the best.

Anon

"My home is not a place; it is people."

Lois McMaster Bujold
Barrayar

"The only way to get a perfect home is to be perfectly happy with the home you've got."
Catherine Fox
How to be Perfect

"Home is the definition of God."

Emily Dickinson

"A good home must be made, not bought."

Joyce Maynard
Domestic Affairs

Honesty

" 'Honesty' without compassion and understanding is not honesty, but subtle hostility."

Rose N Franzblau,
New York Post, 1966

"The elegance of honesty needs no adornment."

Merry Browne

"Honesty is the cornerstone of all success, without which confidence and ability to perform shall cease to exist."

Mary Kay Ash

"I don't mind showing my flaws. It helps other girls realise they can survive."
Angelina Jolie
"Heroine Chic", *Radio Times*,
16–22 August 2003

Hope

"*Flowers grow out of dark moments.*"

Corita Kent

"Dwell in possibility."
Emily Dickinson

"Hope doesn't come from calculating whether the good news is winning out over the bad. It's simply a choice to take action."

Anna Lappe
O Magazine, June 2003

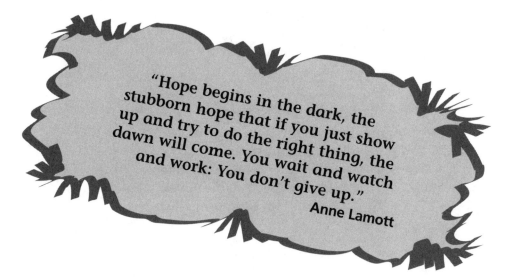

"Hope begins in the dark, the stubborn hope that if you just show up and try to do the right thing, the dawn will come. You wait and watch and work: You don't give up."

Anne Lamott

Housework

"Women, like men, have other interests besides the perennial interests of domesticity."

Virginia Woolf
A Room of One's Own

SPECTACULAR JOB

One day a man spotted a lamp by the roadside. He picked it up, rubbed it vigorously and a genie appeared.

"I'll grant you your fondest wish," the genie said.

The man thought for a moment, then said, "I want a spectacular job – a job that no man has ever succeeded at or has ever attempted to do."

"Poof!" said the genie. "You're a housewife."

"The secret of ironing is to do as little of it as possible."
Shirley Conran

"You can't get spoiled if you do your own ironing."
Meryl Streep

"Housework is a treadmill from futility to oblivion with stop-offs at tedium and counter-productivity."
Erma Bombeck

"My theory on housework is, if the item doesn't multiply, smell, catch on fire or block the refrigerator door – let it be. No one cares. Why should you?"

Erma Bombeck

Humility

"A soul preoccupied with great ideas best performs small duties."

Harriet Martineau

"Don't be humble. You aren't that great."

Golda Meir

"I long to accomplish great and noble tasks, but it is my chief duty to accomplish humble tasks as though they were great and noble. The world is moved along, not only by the mighty shoves of its heroes, but also by the aggregate of the tiny pushes of each honest worker."

Helen Keller

An arrogant, successful businesswoman once told her pastor that there really was no need for her to pray ever again. After all, she had everything – she was young, rich, and good-looking. After hearing this, the pastor said, "Well, you might want to pray for humility."

Source unknown

"If you are humble nothing will touch you, neither praise nor disgrace, because you know what you are."
Mother Teresa

Humour

"Humour is such a strong weapon, such a strong answer. Women have to make jokes about themselves, laugh about themselves, because they have nothing to lose."
Agnes Varda

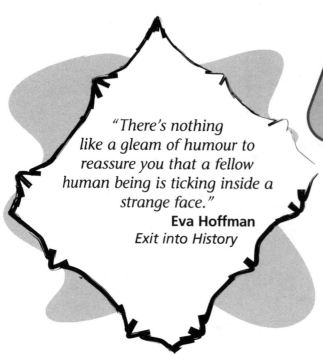

"There's nothing like a gleam of humour to reassure you that a fellow human being is ticking inside a strange face."
Eva Hoffman
Exit into History

"You live but once – you might as well be amusing."
Coco Chanel

"Total absence of humour renders life impossible."
Colette
Chance Acquaintances

"I realise that humour isn't for everyone. It's only for people who want to have fun, enjoy life, and feel alive."

Anne Wilson Schaef

"Humour is a rubber sword – it allows you to make a point without drawing blood."
Mary Hirsch

Husbands

"When I eventually met Mr Right I had no idea that his first name was Always."
Rita Rudner

"A retired husband is often a wife's full-time job."

Ella Harris

"A woman, let her be as good as she may, has got to put up with the life her husband makes for her."
George Eliot
Middlemarch

"Husbands are like fires – they go out if unattended."
Zsa Zsa Gabor

Ideals

"When one paints an ideal, one does not need to limit one's imagination."

Ellen Key

"No man or woman who tries to pursue an ideal in his or her own way is without enemies."

Daisy Bates

"It's really a wonder that I haven't dropped all my ideals, because they seem so absurd and impossible to carry out. Yet I keep them, because in spite of everything I still believe that people are really good at heart."

Anne Frank

Ideas

"No idea is so antiquated that it was not once modern; no idea is so modern that it will not someday be antiquated."

Ellen Glasgow

"A great idea is not enough."

Rosabeth Moss Kanter

"You can kill a man but you can't kill an idea."

Meg Whitman

How do you treat ideas?

Treat them TENDERLY – they can be killed quickly.

Treat them GENTLY – they can be bruised in infancy.

Treat them RESPECTFULLY – they could be the most valuable thing that ever came into your life.

Treat them PROTECTIVELY – don't let them get away.

Treat them NUTRITIONALLY – feed them and feed them well.

Treat them ANTISEPTICALLY – don't let them get infected with the germs of negative thoughts.

Treat them RESPONSIBLY – respond! Do something with them!

Anon

"A healthy hunger for a great idea is the beauty and blessedness of life."
Jean Ingelow

"One clear idea is too precious a treasure to lose."
Caroline Gilman

"If it's a good idea, go ahead and do it. It's much easier to apologise than it is to get permission."
Rear Admiral Grace Murray Hopper

Identity

"The particular human chain we're part of is central to our individual identity."

Elizabeth Stone

Sometimes the best way to figure out who you are is to get to that place where you don't have to be anything else.

Anon

"I think that somehow, we learn who we really are and then live with that decision."

Eleanor Roosevelt

"Definitions belong to the definer, not to the defined."

Toni Morrison

"Normal is in the eye of the beholder."

Whoopi Goldberg

"Women are always being tested ... but ultimately, each of us has to define who we are individually and then do the very best job we can to grow into it."

Hillary Rodham Clinton

"Women are all female impersonators to some degree."

Susan Brownmiller

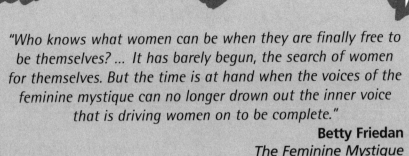

"Who knows what women can be when they are finally free to be themselves? ... It has barely begun, the search of women for themselves. But the time is at hand when the voices of the feminine mystique can no longer drown out the inner voice that is driving women on to be complete."

Betty Friedan
The Feminine Mystique

Imagination

"It is above all by the imagination that we achieve perception and compassion and hope."

Ursula K LeGuin

"All acts performed in the world begin in the imagination."

Barbara Grizzuli Harrison

"Memory feeds imagination."
Amy Tan

"Use your imagination not to scare yourself to death but to inspire yourself to life."

Adele Brookman

"Without leaps of imagination or dreaming, we lose the excitement of possibilities."

Gloria Steinem

Impossibility

"Who so loves, believes the impossible."
Elizabeth Barrett Browning

"This has always been a motto of mine: Attempt the impossible in order to improve your work."
Bette Davis

"All things are possible until they are proved impossible – even the impossible may only be so as of now."
Pearl S Buck

Independence

"I think the girl who is able to earn her own living and pay her own way should be as happy as anybody on earth. The sense of independence and security is very sweet."
Susan B Anthony

"It is easy to be independent when you've got money. But to be independent when you haven't got a thing – that's the Lord's test."

Mahalia Jackson

Initiative

"My mother always told me, 'Never call boys on the telephone. Let them make the first step.' If I'd done that, I'd probably be somebody's secretary right now instead of Secretary of State."
Susan Farmer

"Don't let anyone rob you of your imagination, your creativity, or your curiosity. It's your place in the world; it's your life. Go and do all you can with it, and make it the life you want to live."
Mae Jamison

Inner Life

"After all, it is those who have a deep and real inner life who are best able to deal with the irritating details of outer life."
Evelyn Underhill

"World peace will never be stable until enough of us find inner peace to stabilise it."
Peace Pilgrim

"We must learn to be still in the midst of activity and to be vibrantly alive in repose."
Indira Gandhi

Inspiration

> "I have found that sitting in a place where you have never sat before can be inspiring."
> **Dodie Smith**

"Inspiration usually comes during work, rather than before it."

Madeleine L'Engle

Intelligence

"I happen to feel that the degree of a person's intelligence is directly reflected by the number of conflicting attitudes she can bring to bear on the same topic."
Lisa Alther
Kinflicks

"Many beautiful women have been made happy by their own beauty, but no intelligent woman has ever been made happy by her own intelligence."
Mignon McLaughlin
The Second Neurotic's Notebook

"Brains are an asset, if you hide them."
Mae West

A QUICK TEST OF INTELLIGENCE:

Don't cheat – because if you do, the test will be no fun. I promise there are no tricks to the test.
Read this sentence:

> FINISHED FILES ARE THE RE-
> SULT OF YEARS OF SCIENTIF-
> IC STUDY COMBINED WITH
> THE EXPERIENCE OF YEARS.

Now count aloud the Fs in that sentence. Count them ONLY ONCE: do not go back and count them again. See below ...

Answer:
There are six Fs in the sentence.
A person of average intelligence finds three of them.
If you spotted four you're above average.
If you got five, you can turn your nose up at almost anybody.
If you caught six, you are a genius.

There is no catch. Many people forget the "OF"s. The human brain tends to see them as Vs and not Fs. Pretty weird, don't you think?

Intention

"Each decision we make, each action we take, is born out of an intention."
Sharon Salzberg
"The Power of Intention",
O Magazine, January 2004

"Intentions often melt in the face of unexpected opportunity."
Shirley Temple Black

Interests

"A hobby a day keeps the doldrums away."
Phyllis McGinley

"The effect of having other interests beyond those domestic works well. The more one does and sees and feels, the more one is able to do, and the more genuine may be one's appreciation of fundamental things like home, and love, and understanding companionship."
Amelia Earhart

"One thing life has taught me: if you are interested, you never have to look for new interests. They come to you. When you are genuinely interested in one thing, it will always lead to something else."
Eleanor Roosevelt

"You must learn day by day, year by year to broaden your horizon. The more things you love, the more you are interested in, the more you enjoy, the more you are indignant about, the more you have left when anything happens."
Ethel Barrymore

Jealousy

"Nothing is more capable of troubling our reason, and consuming our health, than secret notions of jealousy in solitude."
Aphra Behn

"Jealousy is all the fun you think they had."
Erica Jong
Fear of Flying

Journaling

"It is not a bad idea to get in the habit of writing down one's thoughts. It saves one having to bother anyone else with them."
Isabel Colegate

"I write entirely to find out what I'm thinking, what I'm looking at, what I see and what it means. What I want and what I fear."
Joan Didion

Joy

"*I cannot believe that the inscrutable universe turns on an axis of suffering; surely the strange beauty of the world must somewhere rest on pure joy!*"

Louise Bogan

"A bird does not sing because it has an answer; it sings because it has a song."

Chinese proverb

"Joy is very infectious; therefore, be always full of joy."

Mother Teresa

"*Joy is a rare plant; it needs much rain for its growth and blossoming.*"

Mrs Charles E Cowman

"*Joy is not gush. Joy is not mere jolly-ness. Joy is perfect acquiescence – acceptance, rest – in God's will, whatever comes. And that is so, only for the soul who delights in God.*"

Amy Carmichael

Justice

"It is not easy to be just."
Rose Elizabeth Bird

"The greatest enemy of justice is privilege."
Marie von Ebner-Eschenbach
Aphorisms

"When it comes to the cause of justice, I take no prisoners and I don't believe in compromise."
Mary Frances Berry

Kindness

"The end result of kindness is that it draws people to you."
Anita Roddick
A Revolution in Kindness

"Each time you step off your path and give someone an act of kindness ... then your road to Happiness just got a little smoother."
Donna A Favors

"As perfume to the flower, so is kindness to speech."
Katherine Francke

"Ask yourself: Have you been kind today? Make kindness your daily *modus operandi* and change your world."
Annie Lennox

"Be kind – remember everyone you meet is fighting a battle – everybody's lonesome."
Marion Parker

"Kindness is always fashionable."
Amelia E Barr

"Sow good services; sweet remembrances will grow them."
Germaine Necker, Madame de Staël

"No kind action ever stops with itself. One kind action leads to another."
Amelia Earhart

"You can't assume that kindness is an inherited trait. It is a learned behaviour."
Katie Couric

Kiss

ONE KISS PER YARD

Walking up to a department store's fabric counter, a pretty girl asked, "I want to buy this material for a new dress. How much does it cost?"

"Only one kiss per yard," replied the smirking male clerk.

"That's fine," replied the girl. "I'll take ten yards."

With expectation and anticipation written all over his face, the clerk quickly measured out and wrapped the cloth, then teasingly held it out. The girl snapped up the package and pointed to a little old man standing beside her.

She smiled. "Grandpa will pay the bill," she said.

"I married the first man I ever kissed; when I tell this to my children, they just about throw up."
Barbara Bush

The sound of a kiss is much softer than that of a cannon – but its echo lasts a great deal longer.

Anon

"A kiss is a lovely trick designed by nature to stop speech when words become superfluous."
Ingrid Bergman

"A man snatches the first kiss, pleads for the second, demands the third, takes the fourth, accepts the fifth – and endures all the rest."
Helen Rowland

Laughter

> "If you can't make it better, you can laugh at it."
> **Erma Bombeck**

> "Laughter is by definition healthy."
> **Doris Lessing**

> Blessed are those who can laugh at themselves, for they shall never cease to be amused.
> **Anon**

> "Once you can laugh at your own weaknesses, you can move forward."
> **Goldie Hawn**

> "We are able to laugh when we achieve detachment, if only for a moment."
> **May Sarton**

> "We cannot really love anybody with whom we never laugh."
> **Agnes Repplier**
> *Americans and Others*, 1912

> "Life can be wildly tragic at times, and I've had my share. But whatever happens to you, you have to keep a slightly comic attitude. In the final analysis, you have got not to forget to laugh."
> **Katharine Hepburn**

Leadership

"Don't follow the crowd; let the crowd follow you."
Margaret Thatcher

Leadership is the ability to hide your panic from others.
Anon

The best leaders are clear. They continually light the way, and in the process, let each person know that what they do makes a difference.
Anon

"The leadership instinct you are born with is the backbone. You develop the funny bone and the wishbone that go with it."
Elaine Agather

"Leaders must wake people out of inertia; they must get people excited about something they've never seen before, something that does not yet exist."
Rosabeth Moss Kanter

"The secret of a leader lies in the tests she has faced over the whole course of her life and the habit of action she develops in meeting those tests."
Gail Sheehy

"Leaders must pick causes they won't abandon easily, remain committed despite setbacks, and communicate their big ideas over and over again in every encounter."
Rosabeth Moss Kanter

"Assertion is a precondition for leadership."
Michelle Guinness
Woman: The Full Story

Learning

"The basic rule with doctorates is that they have to sound hopelessly – ludicrously ivory-towerish when someone asks you what you are doing. If you wouldn't actually prefer to answer 'Oh, I'm just a housewife', then you are not studying for a proper PhD."
Catherine Fox
How to be Perfect

"One can learn, at least. One can go on learning until the day one is cut off."
Fay Weldon

"There are some things you learn best in calm, and some in storm."
Willa Cather
The Song of the Lark

"If we mean to have heroes, statesmen and philosophers, we should have learned women."

Abigail Adams

"That is what learning is. You suddenly understand something you've understood all your life, but in a new way."

Doris Lessing

The more you study, the more you should have ...

- a GOAL you should be pursuing
- a DREAM you should be launching
- a PLAN you should be executing
- a PROJECT you should be starting
- a POSSIBILITY you should be exploring
- an OPPORTUNITY you should be grabbing
- an IDEA you should be working
- a PROBLEM you should be tackling
- a DECISION you should be making

Anon

Liberation

"There is nothing enlightening about shrinking so that other people will not feel insecure around you ... And as we let our own light shine, we unconsciously give other people permission to do the same. As we are liberated from our own fear, our presence automatically liberates others."

Marianne Williamson

"Fetters of gold are still fetters, and the softest lining can never make them so easy as liberty."
Mary Astell

"Every time we liberate a woman, we liberate a man."
Margaret Mead

"Women's Liberation is just a lot of foolishness. It's the men who are discriminated against. They can't bear children. And no one's likely to do anything about that."

Golda Meir

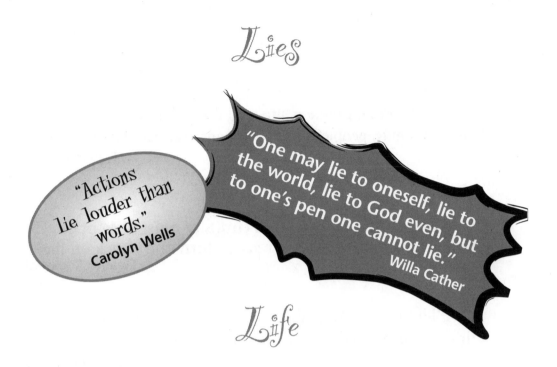

"One may lie to oneself, lie to the world, lie to God even, but to one's pen one cannot lie."
Willa Cather

"Actions lie louder than words."
Carolyn Wells

"I don't believe that life is supposed to make you feel good, or make you feel miserable either. Life is just supposed to make you feel."
Gloria Naylor

"This is all you have. This is not a dry run. This is your life. If you want to fritter it away with your fears, then you will fritter it away, but you won't get it back later."
Laura Schlessinger

"Life is a succession of lessons which must be lived to be understood."
Helen Keller

"I finally figured out the only reason to be alive is to enjoy it."
Rita Mae Brown

"Life is accepting what is, and working from that."
Gloria Naylor

"I believe a worthwhile life is defined by a kind of spiritual journey and a sense of obligation."

Hillary Rodham Clinton

"There is work and there is life, and life should take priority. Life means family, people you love, friends and real relationships."

Esther Rantzen
The Times, 15 July 2003

"Life was meant to be lived and curiosity must be kept alive. One must never, for whatever reason, turn one's back on life."

Eleanor Roosevelt

"Life engenders life. Energy creates energy. It is by spending oneself that one becomes rich."

Sarah Bernhardt

"Life is like a coin. You can spend it any way you wish, but you only spend it once."

Lillian Dickson

"I believe that life should be lived so vividly and so intensely that thoughts of another life, a longer life, are no longer necessary."

Marjory Stoneman Douglas

"Life is what happens when you're making other plans."

Betty Talmadge

"So one thing I want to say about life is: Don't be scared and don't hang back, and most of all, don't waste it."

Joan W Blos

Listening

"With the gift of listening comes the gift of healing."
Catherine de Hueck

"One voice can enter ten ears, but ten voices cannot enter one ear."
Leone Levi

"We learn to listen to our own voices if we are listening at the same time to other women, whose stories, for all our differences, turn out, if we listen well, to be our stories also."
Barbara Deming

"So few people have time to listen, to really listen. This takes time – and time is one of the commodities we are given when we are old."
Elizabeth Basset

Living

"Find ecstasy in life; the mere sense of living is joy enough."
Emily Dickinson

"He lives most life, whoever breathes most air."
Elizabeth Barrett Browning

"People say you should judge whether or not you're alive by whether or not you're breathing, but I disagree with that. I think in order to judge if you are truly alive, you must look at the moments in your life that have taken your breath away."

Michelle Metych
Beloit Daily News, 21 November 2001

Loneliness

"We have all known the long loneliness and we have learned that the only solution is love and that love comes with community."
Dorothy Day

"When we cannot bear to be alone, it means we do not properly value the only companion we will have from birth to death – ourselves."
Eda LeShan

Love

"Love, I find, is like singing. Everyone can do enough to satisfy themselves, though it may not impress the neighbours as being very much."
Zora Neale Hurston

"Love has the innate ability to look past the human and see the godly."
Colette Burnham

"To love is so startling it leaves little time for anything else."
Emily Dickinson

"Love is a choice you make from moment to moment."
Barbara De Angelis

"There is only one path to Heaven. On Earth, we call it Love."
Karen Goldman

"Whoever said love is blind is dead wrong. Love is the only thing that lets us see each other with the remotest accuracy."
Martha Beck
Expecting Adam

"Love works in miracles every day: such as weakening the strong, and strengthening the weak; making fools of the wise, and wise men of fools; favouring the passions, destroying reason, and in a word, turning everything topsy-turvy."
Marguerite de Valois

"Love is not enough. It must be the foundation, the cornerstone – but not the complete structure. It is much too pliable, too yielding."
Bette Davis

"There is no reciprocity. Men love women, women love children, children love hamsters."
Alice Thomas Ellis

"Love cannot survive if you just give it scraps of yourself, scraps of your time, scraps of your thoughts."
Mary O'Hara

"A woman asks little of love: only that she be able to feel like a heroine."
Mignon McLaughlin
The Second Neurotic's Notebook

"If you aren't good at loving yourself, you will have a difficult time loving anyone, since you'll resent the time and energy you give another person that you aren't even giving to yourself."
Barbara De Angelis

"Love does not just sit there, like a stone; it has to be made, like bread, remade all the time, made new."
Ursula K LeGuin

"We are not held back by the love we didn't receive in the past, but by the love we're not extending in the present."
Marianne Williamson
A Return to Love

"Love is everything it's cracked up to be. That's why people are so cynical about it. It really is worth fighting for, being brave for, risking everything for. And the trouble is, if you don't risk anything, you risk even more."
Erica Jong

Manners

> "It is wise to apply the oil of refined politeness to the mechanisms of friendship."
> **Colette**
> *The Pure and the Impure*

"Manners are a sensitive awareness of the feelings of others. If you have that awareness, you have good manners, no matter what fork you use."

Emily Post

Marriage

"A successful marriage requires falling in love many times, always with the same person."
Mignon McLaughlin

"A successful marriage is not a gift; it is an achievement." **Ann Landers**

It starts when you sink in his arms and ends with your arms in his sink.
Anon

"I love being married. It's so great to find that one special person you want to annoy for the rest of your life."
Rita Rudner

"The married are those who have taken the terrible risk of intimacy and, having taken it, know life without intimacy to be impossible."
Carolyn Heilbrun

"A good marriage is one which allows for change and growth in the individuals and in the way they express their love."
Pearl S Buck

"Husband and wife characteristically accept each other as they are. Their faith in each other's regard for them is not based on their own worth or right, but on the other's acceptance of them just as they are."
Esther de Waal
Seeking God

"I used to believe that marriage would diminish me, reduce my options. That you had to be someone less to live with someone else when, of course, you have to be someone more."

Candice Bergen

A good marriage is like a casserole: only those responsible for it really know what goes in it.

Anon

Men

"Men are not the enemy, but the fellow victims. The real enemy is women's denigration of themselves."
Betty Friedan

"Men are simple things. They can survive a whole weekend with only three things: beer, boxer shorts and batteries for the remote control."
Diana Jordan

"Without tenderness, a man is uninteresting."
Marlene Dietrich

"*Give a man a free hand and he'll run it all over you.*"
Mae West

"Man forgives woman anything save the wit to outwit him."
Minna Antrim

"The only thing worse than a man you can't control is a man you can."
Margo Kaufman

"*I know what men want. Men want to be really, really close to someone who will leave them alone.*"
Elayne Boosler

"Never tell a man you can read him through and through; most people prefer to be thought enigmas."
Marchioness Townsend

"Most women tell you that you're a fool if you think you can change a man. But those women are quitters."
"Marge Simpson"

"*I think men who have a pierced ear are better prepared for marriage. They've experienced pain and bought jewellery.*"
Rita Rudner

Men's Rules for Women

If you are cooking a special dinner for a man, be sure to include something from each of the four major male food groups: Meat, Fried, Beer, and Red.

It is only common courtesy that you should leave the seat on the toilet up when you are done.

Don't make him hold your handbag in the shopping centre.

The man is always in charge of the barbecue.

Any attempt by a man to prepare food, no matter how feeble, should be met with roughly the same degree of praise a parent might shower upon their infant when it walks for the first time.

He heard you the first time.

You know, you can ask him out too ...

If you truly want honesty, don't ask questions you don't really want the answer to.

Of course he wants another beer.

Dogs good. Cats bad.

"Fine" is not an acceptable way to end an argument.

Do not question a man's innate navigational abilities by suggesting he stop for directions.

He is the funniest, strongest, best-looking, most successful man you have ever met.

Your bum/boobs/hair/makeup/legs (select appropriate item) look fine. As a matter of fact, it/they look great, so stop asking.

Remember: that Nair bottle looks an awful lot like shampoo if left in the shower.

Dirty laundry comes in several categories: looks fine/smells fine; looks fine/smells bad; Looks dirty/smells fine. Unless you intend to wash it, do not try to disrupt piles organised in this manner.

Yes, Sharon Stone/Pamela Anderson/Cindy Crawford is prettier than you. Just like Brad Pitt/Antonio Banderas/Keanu Reeves is better-looking than him. But since neither one of you is going to be dating any of these people, love the one you're with.

Don't hog the covers.

Watching football is a major turn-on for you. But please wait until the halftime show to act upon that.

Rules that Guys Wished Women Knew

Crying is blackmail.

Ask for what you want. Subtle hints don't work.

Don't cut your hair. Ever.

Sometimes, we're not thinking about you. Live with it.

Get rid of your cat.

Anything we said six or eight months ago is inadmissible in an argument.

Anything you wear is fine. Really.

Christopher Columbus didn't need directions, and neither do we.

You have too many shoes.

If you think you're fat, you probably are. Don't ask us.

Learn to work the toilet seat; if it's up put it down.

Mark anniversaries on a calendar.

Yes, we're bound to miss sometimes.

"Yes" and "No" are perfectly acceptable answers.

A headache that lasts for 17 months is a problem. See a doctor.

Sunday = Sports

If you don't dress like the Victoria's Secret girls, don't expect us to act like soap opera guys.

If something we said can be interpreted two ways, and one of the ways makes you sad and angry, we meant the other one.

If we don't look at other women, how can we know how pretty you are?

You can either ask us to do something OR tell us how you want it done – not both.

Women wearing Wonderbras and low-cut blouses lose their right to complain about having their boobs stared at.

You have enough clothes.

Nothing says "I love you" like sex.

Men and Women

"A man is terribly hampered and partial in his knowledge of women, as a woman in her knowledge of men."
Virginia Woolf
A Room of One's Own

"Men are taught to apologise for their weaknesses, women for their strengths."
Lois Wyse

"Part of the reason that men seem so much less loving than women is that men's behaviour is measured with a feminine ruler."
Francesca Cancian

"Men look *at* themselves in mirrors. Women look *for* themselves."
Elissa Melamed

Women always worry about the things that men forget; men always worry about the things women remember.
Source unknown

"Men enjoy being thought of as hunters, but are generally too lazy to hunt. Women, on the other hand, love to hunt, but would rather nobody knew it."
Mignon McLaughlin
The Second Neurotic's Notebook

"My theory is that men are no more liberated than women."
Indira Gandhi

At the cash dispenser

There are many differences between how a woman and a man uses a drive-through banking machine. Here is his and her cash-dispensing machine usage explained ...

HIS
1. Pull up to dispenser
2. Insert card
3. Enter PIN number and account
4. Take cash, card and receipt
5. Drive away

HERS
1. Pull up to dispenser
2. Check makeup in rear-view mirror
3. Shut off engine
4. Put keys in hand bag
5. Get out of car because you're too far from machine
6. Hunt for card in handbag
7. Insert card
8. Hunt in handbag for wrapper with PIN number written on it
9. Enter PIN number
10. Study instructions for at least two minutes
11. Hit "cancel"
12. Re-enter correct PIN number
13. Check balance
14. Look for envelope
15. Look in handbag for pen
16. Make out deposit slip
17. Endorse cheques
18. Make deposit
19. Study instructions
20. Make cash withdrawal
21. Get in car
22. Check makeup
23. Look for keys
24. Start car
25. Check makeup
26. Start pulling away
27. STOP
28. Back up to machine
29. Get out of car
30. Take card and receipt
31. Get back in car
32. Put card in wallet
33. Put receipt in chequebook
34. Enter deposits and withdrawals in chequebook
35. Clear area in handbag for wallet and chequebook
36. Check makeup
37. Put car in gear; reverse
38. Put car in first gear
39. Drive away from machine
40. Travel three miles
41. Release parking brake

"Women have to be twice as good to get half as far as men."

Agnes MacPhail

"Just as women's bodies are softer than men's, so their understanding is sharper."

Christine de Pisan

Menopause

SIGNS OF MENOPAUSE

1. You sell your central heating system in the Friday free ads.
2. Your husband jokes that instead of buying a wood burning stove, he is using you to heat the sitting room this winter.
3. You have to write Post-it notes with your kids' names on them.
4. You change your underwear after every sneeze.
5. The tweezers you used to use for your eyebrows now get used on your chin.
6. Your brain feels like cotton wool – and it's not a symptom of flu.
7. Those "fat days" seem more frequent – or did you put your favourite skirt in the hot wash without noticing?
8. Your Mother's Day gift is some expensive anti-ageing hand cream – and secretly you're pleased, because you'd never buy it for yourself.
9. Trips to the beauty salon are now essentials, not treats.
10. You find yourself wondering if this is the summer you kiss your bikini days goodbye.

"I refuse to
think of them
as chin hairs. I
think of them
as stray
eyebrows."
Janette Barber

*"You can't get round it. When it
arrives there's a certain kind of
grief because a big, big part of
your life has ended. But with it
there's also a certain relief."*
Julie Walters
Woman and Home, September 2003

Middle Age

"… is when you finally get your head together and your body begins to fall apart."

Caryn Leschen

(oh)

"The really frightening thing about middle age is that you know you'll grow out of it."
Doris Day

Middle age is when you choose your cereal for the fibre, not the toy.

Midlife for women

Midlife is when the growth of the hair on our legs slows down. This gives us plenty of time to care for our newly acquired moustache.

Midlife women no longer have upper arms; we have wingspans. We are no longer women in sleeveless shirts; we are flying squirrels in drag.

Midlife has hit when you stand naked in front of the mirror and can see your rear end without turning around.

Midlife is when you bounce (a lot), but you don't bounce back. It's more like "splat!"

Midlife is when you realise that, if you were a dog, you would need a control-top flea collar.

weeee

Midlife is when you go to the doctor and you realise you are now so old that you have to pay someone to look at you naked.

You know you are getting old when you go for a mammogram and know it is the only time someone will ask you to appear topless in a film.

Midlife brings the wisdom that "life throws you curves" and that you're now sitting on your biggest ones.

Midlife can bring out your angry, bitter side. You look at your latte-swilling, mobile-toting, know-it-all teenager and think, "For this I have stretch marks?"

Midlife is when your memory really starts to go: the only thing you still retain is water.

The good news about midlife is that the glass is still half-full. Of course, the bad news is that it won't be long before your teeth are floating in it.

You know you've crossed the midlife threshold when you're in the supermarket and you hear a Muzak version of "Stairway to Heaven" in the produce department.

Midlife is when you start to repeat yourself and your chins follow suit.

"Turn your midlife crisis to your own advantage by making it a time for renewal of your body and mind, rather than stand by helplessly and watch them decline."
Jane E Brody

"I think women are more interesting in their 40s ... they don't have to be hip and cool any more, which is a godsend."
Jodie Foster

You become more reflective in midlife. You start pondering the "big" questions: what is life, why I am here and how much Healthy Choice ice cream can I eat before it's no longer a healthy choice?

"The fact is, many middle-aged ladies who look 20 years younger than their age show it. A stranger marvelling at the clear smooth skin, unlined throat – is shocked at the age revealed by her thinking."
Dawn Powell
"Dear Diary", *Saga*, August 2003

"Being 50 is ... not knowing more about the world and how it works, but being able to be more of yourself in a very real and expressive way."
Rose Rouse
Woman & Home, July 2003

"And then, not expecting it, you become middle-aged and anonymous. No one notices you; you achieve a wonderful freedom. It's a positive thing – you can move around unnoticed, invisible."
Doris Lessing

"It's nice to have more understanding. You don't play games any more; you grow into yourself and know who you are."
Barbra Streisand
Reader's Digest, November 2003

"Sublime is the domination of the mind over the body, that, for a time, can make flesh and nerve impregnable, and string the sinews like steel so that the weak become so mighty."
Harriet Beecher Stowe

"The most characteristic mark of a great mind is to choose one important object, and pursue it for life."
Anna Letitia Barbauld

"We are commanded to love God with all our minds, as well as with all our hearts, and we commit a great sin if we forbid or prevent that cultivation of the mind in others which would enable them to perform this duty."

Angelina Grimke

Miracles

"Where there is great love, there are always miracles."

Willa Cather

"For the truly faithful, no miracle is necessary. For those who doubt, no miracle is sufficient."

Nancy Gibbs

"Suddenly she was here. And I was no longer pregnant; I was a mother. I never believed in miracles before."

Ellen Greene

Mistakes

"Every great mistake has a halfway moment, a split second when it can be recalled and perhaps remedied."

Pearl S Buck

"I prefer you to make mistakes in kindness than work miracles in unkindness."

Mother Teresa

"Use mis-steps as stepping stones to deeper understanding and greater achievement."

Susan Taylor

"*I make it a policy to try never to make a complete idiot of myself twice in the same way. After all, there are always all kinds of new ways to make a complete idiot of myself. Why repeat the old ones?*"

Margot Dalton

"If I had my life to live over ... I'd dare to make more mistakes next time."

Nadine Stair

"It is so conceited and timid to be ashamed of one's mistakes."

Brenda Ueland

Moment

"*It is only when we truly know and understand that we have a limited time on earth – and that we have no way of knowing when our time is up that we will begin to live each day to the fullest, as if it was the only one we had.*"

Elisabeth Kübler-Ross

"Life is a succession of moments. To live each one is to succeed."
Corita Kent

"We are here for so short a while. Savour the moment as it passes. This is your shining hour – all the glory of the universe is yours."
Pam Brown

"Learning to live in the present moment is part of the path of joy."
Sarah Ban Breathnach

"Love the moment, and the energy of that moment will spread beyond all boundaries."
Corita Kent

"Sometimes I would almost rather have people take away years of my life than take away a moment."
Pearl Bailey

"I'm trying to be in the moment, and I'm enjoying life."
Barbra Streisand
Reader's Digest, November 2003

Money

"Money is the root of all evil, and yet it is such a useful root that we cannot get on without it any more than we can without potatoes."
Louisa May Alcott

"Money is a good servant, but a poor master."

Dominique Bouhours

"Girls just want to have funds."
Adrienne E Gusoff

"To fulfil a dream, to be allowed to sweat over lonely labour, to be given the chance to create, is the meat and potatoes of life. The money is the gravy. As everyone else, I love to dunk my crust in it. But alone, it is not a diet designed to keep body and soul together."

Bette Davis
The Lonely Life

"If you think a million dollars will solve all your problems, you've never had a million dollars."

Marianne Williamson

"It's better to do nothing with your money than something you don't understand."

Suze Orman
O Magazine, February 2003

"Having money is rather like being a blonde. It's more fun but not vital."
Mary Quant

"It is more rewarding to watch money change the world than watch it accumulate."

Gloria Steinem

"Not earning much is a liberation. You always spend up to the amount you have – so if you have less, you spend less."
Lynne Watts
Good Housekeeping, April 2004

"I am not interested in money. I just want to be wonderful."
Marilyn Monroe

Mothers

"And so our mothers and grandmothers have, more often than not anonymously, handed on the creative spark, the seed of the flower they themselves never hoped to see – or like a sealed letter they could not plainly read."
Alice Walker

"I know how to do anything – I'm a mum."
Roseanne Barr

"When I stopped seeing my mother with the eyes of a child, I saw the woman who helped me give birth to myself."
Nancy Friday

Things that could have been said by mums in the Bible

Samson! Get your hand out of that lion – you don't know where it's been!

David! I told you not to play in the house with that sling! Go practise your harp. We pay good money for those lessons!

Abraham! Stop wandering around the countryside and get home for supper!

Shadrach, Meshach and Abednego! Leave those clothes outside – you smell like you've been mucking about with a bonfire!

Cain! Get off your brother! You're going to kill him some day!

Noah! No, you can't keep them! I told you, don't bring home any more strays!

Gideon! Just look at the state of you! Have you been hiding in that winepress again?

James, John! No more burping contests at the dinner table, please. People are going to call you the sons of thunder!

Judas! Have you been in my purse again?!

"What do girls do who haven't any mothers to help them through their troubles?"
Louisa May Alcott

"All mothers are physically handicapped. They have only two hands."

Julie Andrews
The Best of Bits and Pieces

"Some mothers are kissing mothers and some are
scolding mothers, but it is love just the same,
and most mothers kiss and scold together."

Pearl S Buck

"She never quite leaves her children at home,
even when she doesn't take them along."

Margaret Culkin Banning

*"When you are a mother, you are never really alone in your thoughts.
A mother always has to think twice, once for herself and once for her child."*

Sophia Loren
Women and Beauty

"Motherhood has a very humanising effect.
Everything gets reduced to essentials."

Meryl Streep

*"Mother love is the fuel that enables a normal
human being to do the impossible."*

Marion C Garretty

***"Mother love makes a woman more vulnerable
than any other creature on earth."***

Pam Brown

"Any mother could perform the jobs of several
air traffic controllers with ease."

Lisa Alther

The following are different answers given by school-age children to the given questions:

Why did God make mothers?
1. She's the only one who knows where the sticky tape is.
2. Think about it, it was the best way to get more people.
3. Mostly to clean the house.
4. To help us out of there when we were getting born.

How did God make mothers?
1. He used dirt, just like for the rest of us.
2. Magic plus super powers and a lot of stirring.
3. He made my mum just the same like he made me. He just used bigger parts.

Why did God give you your mother and not some other mum?
1. We're related.
2. God knew she likes me a lot more than other people's mums like me.

What ingredients are mothers made of?
1. God makes mothers out of clouds and angel hair and everything nice in the world, and one dab of mean.
2. They had to get their start from men's bones. Then they mostly use string. I think.

What kind of little girl was your mum?
1. My mum has always been my mum and none of that other stuff.
2. I don't know because I wasn't there, but my guess would be pretty bossy.
3. They say she used to be nice.

What did mum need to know about dad before she married him?
1. His last name.
2. She had to know his background. Like is he a crook?
3. Does he get drunk on beer? Did he say "No" to drugs and "Yes" to chores?

Why did your mum marry your dad?
1. My dad makes the best spaghetti in the world. And my mum eats a lot.
2. She got too old to do anything else with him.
3. My grandma says that mum didn't have her thinking cap on.

Who's the boss at your house?
1. Mum doesn't want to be boss, but she has to because Dad's such a goofball.

2. Mum. You can tell by room inspection. She sees the stuff under the bed.
3. I guess Mum is, but only because she has a lot more to do than dad.

What's the difference between mums and dads?
1. Mums work at work and work at home, and dads just get to work at work.
2. Mums know how to talk to teachers without scaring them.
3. Dads are taller and stronger, but mums have all the real power 'cause that's who I've got to ask if I want to sleep over at my friend's.

What does your mum do in her spare time?
1. Mothers don't do spare time.
2. To hear her tell it, she pays bills all day long.

What's the difference between mums and grandmas?
1. About 30 years.
2. You can always count on grandmothers for sweets. Sometimes mums don't even have bread on them!

Describe the world's greatest mum.
1. She would make broccoli taste like ice cream!
2. The greatest mum in the world wouldn't make me kiss my fat aunts!
3. She'd always be smiling and keep her opinions to herself.

Is anything about your mum perfect?
1. Her teeth are perfect, but she bought them from the dentist.
2. Her casserole recipes. But we hate them.
3. Just her children.

What would it take to make your mum perfect?
1. On the inside she's already perfect. Outside, I think some kind of plastic surgery.
2. Diet. You know her hair. I'd dye-it, maybe blue.

If you could change one thing about your mum, what would it be?
1. She has this weird thing about me keeping my room clean. I'd get rid of that.
2. I'd make my mum smarter. Then she would know it was my sister who did it and not me.

"The phrase 'working mother' is redundant."
Jane Sellman

"A mother is a person who, seeing there are only four pieces of pie for five people, promptly announces she never did care for pie."
Tenneva Jordan

"Now, as always, the most automated appliance in a household is the mother."
Beverly Jones

Nature

"Nature is the most beautiful
thing we have. It's better than art
because it's from the Creator."
Olivia Newton-John

"The earth is the very
quintessence of the
human condition."
Hannah Arendt
The Human Condition

*"The more clearly we can focus our
attention on the wonders and realities
of the universe about us, the less taste
we shall have for destruction."*
Rachel Carson
Silent Spring

Needs

*"Many of our troubles in the world
today arise from an over-emphasis of
the masculine, and a neglect of the
feminine. This modern world is an
aggressive, hyperactive, competitive, masculine
world, and it needs the woman's touch as never before."*
Eva Burrows

"What
the world really
needs is more love and
less paperwork."
Pearl Bailey

New

> "At first people refuse to believe that a strange new thing can be done, then they begin to hope that it can be done, then they see that it can be done – then it is done and all the world wonders why it was not done centuries ago."
>
> **Frances Hodgson Burnett**

"Just because a book is new doesn't mean it contains more pleasure and wisdom than an old one."

Libby Purves
Saga, August 2003

"Hold a book in your hand and you're a pilgrim at the gates of a new city."

Anne Michaels
Fugitive Pieces

"My cancer scare changed my life. I'm grateful for every new, healthy day I have. It has helped me prioritise my life."

Olivia Newton-John

"If we would have new knowledge, we must get a whole world of new questions."

Susanne K Langer

"True originality consists not in a new manner but in a new vision."

Edith Wharton
The Writing of Fiction

"So never lose an opportunity of urging a practical beginning, however small, for it is wonderful how often in such matters the mustard-seed germinates and roots itself."

Florence Nightingale

Nothing

"There is no pleasure in having nothing to do;
the fun is in having lots to do and not doing it."
Mary Wilson Little

"I don't wait for moods. You accomplish
nothing if you do that. Your mind must
know it has got to get down to work."
Pearl S Buck

"Nothing great is ever
accomplished by one person."
Sheryl Leach
creator of Barney the Dinosaur

"The main dangers in this
life are the people who want
to change everything ... or
nothing."
Lady Nancy Astor

"Nothing is interesting
if you're not
interested."
Helen MacInness

"People don't resent having nothing
nearly as much as too little."
Ivy Compton-Burnett

"As for me, prizes mean nothing;
my prize is my work."
Katharine Hepburn
quoted in the *Telegraph*, 30 June 2003

"If you do nothing unexpected, nothing unexpected happens."
Fay Weldon

Don't get your knickers in a knot; nothing is solved and it just makes you walk funny.
Source unknown

Nudity

"There are few nudities so objectionable as the naked truth."
Agnes Repplier

"It's not true that I had nothing on. I had the radio on."
Marilyn Monroe

"After 30, a body has a mind of its own."
Source unknown

"Curve: the loveliest distance between two points."
Mae West

"A waist is a terrible thing to mind."
Jane Caminos

"I decided I wouldn't let my body shape become an all-encompassing part of my life. There are other things you can do to improve your personal sense of self-worth."
Tanni Grey Thompson
Good Housekeeping, September 2003

"I'm just a person trapped inside a woman's body."
Elaine Boosler

Obstacles

"Obstacles are those frightful things you see when you take your eyes off the goal."

Hannah Moore

"Obstacles often are not personal attacks; they are muscle-builders."

Anne Wilson Schaef

"We can be negative and cynical or we can be charged and hot-wired to find a way through it, over it, around it, under it."

Laura Schlessinger

Opportunity

"*Civil Rights opened the windows. When you open the windows, it does not mean that everybody will get through. We must create our own opportunities.*"

Mary Frances Berry

"Posterity is full of men who seized the day while women were planning for a fortnight on Tuesday."
Allison Pearson
I Don't Know How She Does It

"Opportunities are usually disguised as hard work, so most people don't recognise them."
Ann Landers

"You have to recognise when the right place and the right time fuse, and take advantage of that opportunity. There are plenty of opportunities out there. You can't sit back and wait."
Ellen Metcalf

"When one door of happiness closes, another opens; but often we look so long at the closed door that we do not see the one which has been opened for us."
Helen Keller

The door to opportunity is always labelled "push".
Anon

Oppression

"When men are oppressed, it's tragedy; when women are oppressed, it's tradition."

Bernadette Mosala

"No person is your friend, who demands your silence, or denies your right to grow."

Alice Walker

"Oppression involves a failure of the imagination: the failure to imagine the full humanity of other human beings."

Margaret Atwood

Optimism

"I have become my own version of an optimist. If I can't make it through one door, I'll go through another door – or I'll make a door. Something terrific will come, no matter how dark the present."

Joan Rivers

"The real winners in life are the people who look at every situation with an expectation that they can make it work or make it better."

Barbara Hetcher

There is no danger of developing eyestrain from looking on the bright side of things.

Anon

"An optimist is the human personification of Spring."

Susan J Bissonette

Organisation

"A schedule defends from chaos and whim."
Annie Dillard

"Order is the shape upon which beauty depends."
Pearl S Buck
To My Daughters, With Love

"Life's a lot easier when you know where to find things."
Melanie Cantor
Quoted in "Freedom is a black sack", *Radio Times*, 6–12 March 2004

"Don't agonise. Organise."
Florence Kennedy

"Life is too complicated not to be orderly."
Martha Stewart

Passion

"Each of us has a fire in our hearts for something. It's our goal in life to find it and keep it lit."
Mary Lou Retton

"The inner fire is the most important thing mankind possesses."
Edith Sodergran

"Passion is timeless and priceless."
Jill Leiber

Past

"There is a way to look at the past. Don't hide from it. It will not catch you – if you don't repeat it."
Pearl Bailey

"We can never go back and do yesterday; we can only learn from it and do a better tomorrow."
Anne Wilson Schaef

"Accept your past – don't deny it. If you carry forward old regrets and resentments you'll remain bound by them. Making peace with the past stops it clouding your present or dictating your future."

Fiona Harrold
"Re-invent Yourself from the Inside Out",
Good Housekeeping, April 2004

"Our past is a story existing only in our minds. Look, analyse, understand, and forgive. Then as quickly as possible, chuck it."
Marianne Williamson

Never look back unless you are planning to go that way.

Anon

"That it will never come again is what makes life so sweet."

Emily Dickinson

Patience

"It is strange that the years teach us patience; that the shorter our time, the greater our capacity for waiting."
Elizabeth Taylor

Peace

"Peace has to be created, in order to be maintained. It is the product of Faith, Strength, Energy, Will, Sympathy, Justice, Imagination, and the triumph of principle. It will never be achieved by passivity and quietism."
Dorothy Thompson

"We receive His peace when we ask Him for it. We keep His peace by extending it to others. Those are the keys and there are no others."
Marianne Williamson

"Peace, like every other rare and precious thing, doesn't come to you. You have to go and get it."
Faith Forsyte

"For it isn't enough to talk about peace. One must believe it. And it isn't enough to believe in it. One must work at it. The future belongs to those who believe in the beauty of their dreams."
Eleanor Roosevelt

Peace is the deliberate adjustment of my life to the will of God.
Anon

Perfectionism

"I don't confuse greatness with perfection. To be great anyhow is ... the higher achievement."
Lois McMaster Bujold
Mirror Dance

"In order to go on living one must try to escape the death involved in perfectionism."
Hannah Arendt
Rachel Varnhagen

"Striving for excellence motivates you; striving for perfection is demoralising."
Harriet Braiker

"Maybe the most any of us can expect of ourselves isn't perfection but progress."
Michelle Burford
O Magazine, 2003

"You will never be perfect. But you can be better than you are now. For your own sake, try."
Nancy Wood
Dancing Moons

"Perfection does not exist in doing extraordinary things, but in doing ordinary things extraordinarily well."

Angelique Arnauld

Perseverance

"What keeps you going isn't some fine destination, but the road you're on, and the fact you know how to drive."
Barbara Kingsolver

"One of the sources of pride in being a human being is the ability to bear present frustrations in the interests of longer purposes."
Helen Merrell Lynd

"I have never been especially impressed by the heroics of people who are convinced they are about to change the world. I am more awed by those who struggle to make one small difference after another."
Ellen Goodman

"Perseverance is failing 19 times and succeeding the 20th."
Julie Andrews

Perspective

"If you look at life one way, there is always cause for alarm."
Elizabeth Bowen

"The beautiful seems right by force of beauty and the feeble wrong because of weakness."
Elizabeth Barrett Browning

"If you see a whole thing – it seems it's always beautiful. Planets, lives ... But close up, a world's all dirt and rocks. And day to day, life's a hard job, you get tired, you lose the pattern."

Ursula K LeGuin

"We don't see things as they are; we see them as we are."

Anaïs Nin

"Never let a problem to be solved become more important than the person to be loved."

Barbara Johnson

"Remember that you have only one soul; that you have only one death to die; that you have only one life … If you do this, there will be many things about which you care nothing."

St Teresa of Avila

"A small trouble is like a pebble. Hold it too close to your eye and it fills the whole world and puts everything out of focus. Hold it at a proper distance and it can be examined and properly classified. Throw it at your feet and it can be seen in its true setting, just one more tiny bump on the pathway of life."

Celia Luce

Pets

"Did you ever walk into a room and forget why you walked in? I think that's how dogs spend their lives."
Sue Murphy

I was driving by a pet shop when I noticed a sign saying, "All birds going cheap".

A Cat's Diary

Day 751: My captors continue to torment me with bizarre, dangling objects. They eat lavish meals in my presence while I am forced to subsist on dry cereal. The only thing that keeps me going is the hope of eventual escape – that, and the satisfaction I get from occasionally ruining some piece of their furniture.

I fear I may be going insane. Yesterday, I ate a houseplant. Tomorrow I may eat another.

"Dogs are wise. They crawl away into a quiet corner and lick their wounds and do not rejoin the world until they are whole once more."
Agatha Christie

Things Dogs Must Try To Remember

I will not play tug-of-war with Dad's underwear when he's on the toilet.

The dustbin man is NOT stealing our stuff.

I do not need to suddenly stand straight up when I'm lying under the coffee table.

I will not roll my toys behind the fridge.

I must shake the rainwater out of my fur BEFORE entering the house.

I will not eat the cats' food, before or after they eat it.

I will stop trying to find the few remaining pieces of clean carpet in the house when I am about to throw up.

I will not throw up in the car.

I will not roll on dead seagulls, fish, crabs, etc.

I will not eat any more socks and then redeposit them in the backyard after processing.

I will not chew my human's toothbrush and not tell them.

I will not chew crayons or pens, especially not the red ones, or my people will think I am haemorrhaging.

When in the car, I will not insist on having the window rolled down when it's raining outside.

We do not have a doorbell. I will not bark each time I hear one on TV.

I will not steal Mum's underwear and dance all over the backyard with it.

The sofa is not a face towel.

My head does not belong in the refrigerator.

I will not bite the officer's hand when he reaches for Mum's driver's licence.

Does Your Cat Own You?

At the supermarket, do you pick up the cat food and cat litter before you pick out anything for yourself?

Did you buy a video tape of fish swimming in an aquarium to entertain your cat?

Do the Christmas cards you send out feature your cat sitting on Santa's lap? Does your cat sign the card?

Do you admit to non-cat owners how many cats you really have?

Do you climb out of bed over the headboard or footboard, so you won't disturb the sleeping cat?

Do you cook a special turkey for your cat on holidays?

Do you feed your cat tidbits from the table with your fork?

Do you give your cat presents and a stocking at Christmas?

Do you have more than four opened but rejected cans of cat food in the refrigerator?

Do you have pictures of your cat in your wallet? Do you bring them out when your friends share pictures of their children?

Do you kiss your cat on the lips?

Do you microwave your cat's food? Prepare it from scratch?

Do you put off making the bed until the cat gets up?

Do you scoop out the litter box after each use? Do you wait at the box with the scoop in your hand?

Do you sleep in the same position all night because it annoys your cats when you move?

Do you think it's cute when your cat swings on the drapes or licks the butter?

Does your cat sit at the table (or ON the table) when you eat?

Does your desire to collect cats intensify during times of stress?

When people call to talk to you on the phone, do you insist that they say a few words to your cat as well?

When someone new comes to your house, do you introduce your cat, by name, to them?

Will you stand at the open door indefinitely in the freezing rain while your cat sniffs the door, deciding whether to go out or come in?

Would you rather spend a night at home with your cat than go out on a bad date?

Plans

"It takes as much energy to wish as it does to plan."
Eleanor Roosevelt

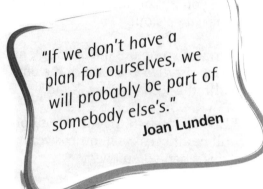

"If we don't have a plan for ourselves, we will probably be part of somebody else's."
Joan Lunden

"Forethought spares afterthought."
Amelia Barr
Jen Vedder's Wife

Pleasure

"Beware of over-great pleasure in being popular or even beloved."
Margaret Fuller

"It isn't the great big pleasures that count the most; it's making a great deal out of the little ones."
Jean Webster

"Variety is the soul of pleasure."
Aphra Behn

PMS

Top ten things PMS stands for

10. Psychotic Mood Shift
9. Pack My Stuff
8. Perpetual Munching Spree
7. Puffy Mid-Section
6. People Make me Sick
5. Provide Me with Sweets
4. Pardon My Sobbing
3. Pimples May Surface
2. Pass My Sweatpants
1. Plainly Men Suck

"My licence plate says PMS ... Nobody cuts me off."
Wendy Leibman

They call it PMS ... because Mad Cow Disease was already taken.

Anon

Politics

"The pursuit of politics is religion, morality, and poetry all in one."
Germaine Necker, Madame de Staël

"The reason there are so few female politicians is that it is too much trouble to put makeup on two faces."
Maureen Murphy

"Everybody's for democracy in principle. It's only in practice that the thing gives rise to stiff objections."
Meg Greenfield

"I've always said that in politics, your enemies can't hurt you, but your friends will kill you."
Ann Richards

Possessions

"I am happy to live frugally. I have found the whole experience liberating."
Carole Luby
"Living in a Box",
Sunday Telegraph,
28 March 2004

"Spoiled. That's all it's about – can't live without this, can't live without that. You can live without anything you weren't born with, and you can make it through on even half of that."
Gloria Naylor

Appreciate what you have

One day … a wealthy woman took her daughter on a trip to the country, so she could have her see how poor country people live.

They stayed one day and one night in the home of a very humble farmer. At the end of the trip, and when they were back home, the woman asked her daughter, "What did you think of the trip?"

The daughter replied, "Very nice, Mummy."

"Did you notice how poor the people were?" asked the mother.

"Yes," said the girl.

"So what did you learn?"

The daughter responded, "I learned that we have one dog in our house, and they have four. Also, we have a fountain in our garden, but they have a stream that has no end.

And we have imported lamps in our garden … where they have the stars! And our garden goes to the edge of our property. But they have the entire horizon as their back garden!"

At the end of her daughter's reply the mother was speechless. The girl then said, "Thank you, Mum, for showing me how poor we really are."

Possibilities

"The possible's slow fuse is lit by the imagination."
Emily Dickinson

"The possibilities are numerous once we decide to act and not to react."
Gloria Anzaldua

"Don't be obsessed with the idea that there is only one possibility. If you think so, there is only one."
Katharine Butler Hathaway
The Journals and Letters of the Little Locksmith

Power

"Arbitrary power is like most other things which are very hard: very liable to be broken."

Abigail Adams

"If [women] understood and exercised their power they could remake the world."

Emily Taft Douglas

"To deny we need and want power is to deny that we hope to be effective."

Liz Smith

"The thing women have yet to learn is that nobody gives you power. You just take it."

Roseanne Barr

"Power corrupts indeed when the weak band together in order to ruin the strong, but not before."

Hannah Arendt

Prayer

"Prayer is essentially a love affair with God."

Mother Mary Clare

"Prayer is nothing else than being on terms of friendship with God."
St Teresa of Avila

"Perfect prayer seeks the [incarnate] presence of Christ and recognises it in every human face."
Catherine de Hueck Doherty

"*Prayer is more than meditation. In meditation, the source of strength is one's self. When one prays, he goes to a source of strength greater than his own.*"
Germaine Necker, Madame de Staël

"An authentic life is the most personal form of worship. Everyday life has become my prayer."
Sarah Ban Breathnach

"If we pray, we will believe; if we believe we will love; if we love, we will serve."
Mother Teresa

A Woman's Prayer

Dear Lord,
So far today, I am doing all right.
I have not gossiped, lost my temper,
been greedy, grumpy, nasty, selfish, or self-indulgent.
I have not whined, sworn, or eaten any chocolate.
I have not charged my credit card.
However, I am going to get out of bed in a few
minutes and I will need a lot more help after that.
Amen.

Prejudice

"Nobody outside of a baby carriage or a judge's chamber believes in an unprejudiced point of view."
Lillian Hellman

Prejudice is being down on something you're not up on.
Anon

"Choose your friends by their character and your socks by their colour. Choosing your socks by their character makes no sense, and choosing your friends by their colour is unthinkable."
Julie Andrews

Progress

"I was taught that the way of progress is neither swift nor easy."
Marie Curie

"People want progress, but they don't want change."
Eva Burrows

"We haven't come a long way; we've come a short way. If we hadn't come a short way, no one would be calling us 'baby'."
Elizabeth Janeway

"The human mind always makes progress, but it is progress in spirals."
Germaine Necker, Madame de Staël

"Every generation must go further than the last or what's the use in it?"
Meridel Le Sueur

Purpose

"God has a special purpose for each one of us. He will open up all sorts of possibilities for us if we place our lives in his hands and ask him to guide us."
Beth Spring
Childless: The Hurt and the Hope

"Learn to get in touch with the silence within yourself, and know that everything in life has purpose. There are no mistakes, no coincidences; all events are blessings given to us to learn from."
Elisabeth Kübler-Ross

Ever Wonder Why?

Why the sun lightens our hair, but darkens our skin?

Why women can't put on mascara with their mouths closed?

Why don't you ever see the headline "Psychic Wins Lottery"?

Why is "abbreviated" such a long word?

Why is it that doctors call what they do "practice"?

Why is it that to stop Windows XP, you have to click on "Start"?

Why is lemon juice made with artificial flavour, and dishwashing liquid made with real lemons?

Why is the person who invests all your money called a broker?

Why is the time of day with the slowest traffic called rush hour?

Why isn't there mouse-flavoured cat food?

Why is it good if a vacuum really sucks?

Why didn't Noah swat those two mosquitoes?

Why do they sterilise the needle for lethal injections?

Why don't sheep shrink when it rains?

Why are they called apart-ments when they are all stuck together?

If flying is so safe, why do they call the airport the terminal?

Doesn't expecting the unexpected make the unexpected expected?

When dog food is new and improved-tasting, who tests it?

Why can a pizza get to your house faster than an ambulance?

Why do supermarkets make sick people walk all the way to the back of the shop to get their prescriptions while healthy people can buy cigarettes at the front?

Why do people order double cheeseburgers, large fries, and a DIET coke?

Why do banks leave both doors open and chain the pens to the counters?

Why do we leave cars worth thousands of pounds on the drive and lock our junk and cheap lawnmower in the garage?

Why do we use answering machines to screen calls and then have call waiting so we won't miss a call from someone we didn't want?

"Some questions don't have answers, which is a terribly difficult lesson to learn."
Katharine Graham

"The power to question is the basis of all human progress."
Indira Gandhi

Quotations

"I love quotations because it is a joy to find thoughts one might have, beautifully expressed with much authority by someone recognised wiser than oneself."
Marlene Dietrich

"I always have a quotation for everything – it saves original thinking."
Dorothy Sayers

"If you have any doubts that we live in a society controlled by men, try reading down the index of contributors to a volume of quotations, looking for women's names."
Elaine Gill

"I would venture to guess that Anon, who wrote so many poems without signing them, was often a woman."
Virginia Woolf

"Quotations can be valuable, like raisins in the rice pudding, for adding iron as well as eye appeal."
Peg Bracken
I Didn't Come Here to Argue

Reality

"It is in the knowledge of the genuine conditions of our lives that we must draw our strength to live and our reasons for living."

Simone de Beauvoir

"The camera makes everyone a tourist in other people's reality, and eventually in one's own."

Susan Sontag
New York Review of Books, 18 April 1974

"Reality is nothing but a collective hunch."
Lily Tomlin

"Reality is the leading cause of stress amongst those in touch with it."

Jane Wagner

"The people who say you are not facing reality actually mean that you are not facing their idea of reality. Reality is above all else a variable. With a firm enough commitment, you can sometimes create a reality which did not exist before."

Margaret Halsey
No Laughing Matter

BARBIE: GET REAL!

It's about time Barbie got real. Now, at long last, here are some NEW Barbie dolls to coincide with her ageing:

Bifocals Barbie: Comes with her own set of blended-lens fashion frames in six wild colours (half-frames, too!), neck chain and large-print editions of Vogue and Country Living.

Hot Flush Barbie: Press Barbie's bellybutton and watch her face turn beetroot red while tiny drops of perspiration appear on her forehead. Hand-held mini-fan and tiny tissues included.

Facial Hair Barbie: As Barbie's hormone levels shift, see her whiskers grow. Available with teensy tweezers and magnifying mirror.

Flabby Arms Barbie: Hide Barbie's droopy triceps with these new, roomier-sleeved gowns. Good news on the tummy front: two girdles with tummy-support panels are included.

Bunion Barbie: Years of disco dancing in stiletto heels have definitely taken their toll on Barbie's dainty arched feet. Soothe her sores with the pumice stone and plasters, and then slip on soft terry mules.

No-More Wrinkles Barbie: Erase those pesky crow's-feet and lip lines with a tube of Skin Sparkle-Spackle, from Barbie's own line of exclusive age-blasting cosmetics.

Soccer Mum Barbie: All that experience as a cheerleader is really paying off as Barbie dusts off her old high school megaphone to root for Babs and Ken Jr. Comes with minivan in robin-egg blue or white, and cooler filled with doughnut holes and fruit punch.

Post-menopausal Barbie: This Barbie spots when she sneezes, forgets where she puts things and cries a lot. She is sick and tired of Ken sitting on the couch watching the tube, clicking through the channels. Comes with TenaLady and Kleenex.

Divorced Barbie: Comes with Ken's house, Ken's car and Ken's boat and self-help back-to-work manual.

Regret

"Never regret. If it's good, it's wonderful. If it's bad, it's experience."
Victoria Holt

"At the end of your life, you will never regret not having passed one more test, not winning one more verdict or not closing one more deal. You will regret time not spent with a husband, a friend, a child, or a parent."
Barbara Bush

"I don't like to think about regrets. And if by chance they should creep up on you, you should put them behind your shoulder."
Sophia Loren
Sunday Times Magazine, 21 June 2003

Relationships

"Intimate relationships cannot substitute for a life plan. But to have any meaning or viability at all, a life plan must include intimate relationships."
Harriet Lerner

"There are people whom one loves immediately and forever. Even to know they are alive in the world with one is quite enough."
Nancy Spain

"One part of persevering in any loving relationship is allowing the other person room to be themselves and to grow."
Esther de Waal
Seeking God: The Way of St Benedict

"Cherish your human connections – your relationships with friends and family."
Barbara Bush

Relaxation

"There is no need to go to India or anywhere else to find peace. You will find that deep place of silence right in your room, your garden or even your bathtub."
Elisabeth Kübler-Ross

"Put duties aside at least an hour before bed and perform soothing, quiet activities that will help you relax."
Dianne Hales

"When in doubt take a bath. It can calm your mind, relax your tired, tense body, and soothe your stressed soul. Baths are necessary for spiritual replenishment and centring as a prayer and meditation."
Sarah Ban Breathnach

Renewal

"There is nothing like a newborn baby to renew your spirit –
and to buttress your resolve to make the world a better place."
Virginia Kelley

*"You've got to make a conscious choice every day to shed
the old – whatever 'the old' means for you."*
Sarah Ban Breathnach

"Sometimes you've got to let everything go – purge yourself.
If you are unhappy with anything … whatever is bringing you
down, get rid of it. Because you'll find that when you're free,
your true creativity – your true self comes out."
Tina Turner

*"Personal transformation can and does have global effects.
As we go, so goes the world, for the world is us. The revolution
that will save the world is ultimately a personal one."*
Marianne Williamson

"It now seems to me that one changes from day to day
and that every few years one becomes a new being."
George Sand

Reputation

A good name, like good will, is attained by many actions and may be lost by one.

Anon

"Nothing is so delicate as the reputation of a woman; it is at once the most beautiful and most brittle of all human things."

Jane Welsh Carlyle

"Reputation is what other people know about you. Honour is what you know about yourself ... Guard your honour. Let your reputation fall where it will."

Lois McMaster Bujold
A Civil Campaign

"No man can understand why a woman shouldn't prefer a good reputation to a good time."

Helen Rowland

Response

"If you give your life as a wholehearted response to love, then love will wholeheartedly respond to you."
Marianne Williamson

"If you can react the same way to winning and losing, that's a big accomplishment. That quality is important because it stays with you the rest of your life."

Chris Evert

It's not what happens to people that's important. It's what they do about it.
Anon

Responsibility

"I believe that we are solely responsible for our choices, and we have to accept the consequences of every deed, word, and thought throughout our lifetime."
Elisabeth Kübler-Ross

"Dreading your responsibilities can use up more time and energy than fulfilling them."
Woman & Home,
October 2003

"Nothing strengthens the judgement and quickens the conscience like individual responsibility."
Elizabeth Cady Stanton

"We are responsible for the quality of our vision, we have a say in the shaping of our sensibility. In the many thousand daily choices we make, we create ourselves and the voice with which we speak and work."
Carolyn Forche

Revenge

"People who fight
fire with fire usually
end up with ashes."
Abigail Van Buren

*"The only people with
whom you should try
to get even are those
who have helped you."*
Mae Maloo

Revolution

"Revolution begins
with the self, in the
self."

Toni Cade Bambara

*"The first duty of a
revolutionary is to get
away with it."*
Abbie Hoffman

*"Revolution
is not a onetime
event."*
Audre Lorde

"The most radical
revolutionary will become
a conservative the day
after the revolution."
Hannah Arendt

*"The greatest revolution in our generation
is that of human beings, who by changing
the inner attitudes of their minds, can
change the outer aspects of their lives."*
Marilyn Ferguson

Right

"Some feminists feel that a woman should never be wrong. We have a right to be wrong."

Alice Childress

"The right way is not always the popular and easy way. Standing for right when it is unpopular is a true test of moral character."
Margaret Chase Smith

"Do what you feel in your heart to be right, for you'll be criticised anyway. You'll be damned if you do and damned if you don't."
Eleanor Roosevelt

"The reward for doing right is mostly an internal phenomenon: self-respect, dignity, integrity, and self-esteem."

Laura Schlessinger

Rights

"If women want any rights they had better take them and say nothing about it."

Harriet Beecher Stowe

"Nobody can argue any longer about women's rights. It's like arguing about the rights of earthquakes."

Lillian Hellman

"You are a human being. You have rights inherent in that reality. You have dignity and worth that exist prior to law."

Lyn Beth Neylon

Risk

"In order for people to be happy, sometimes they have to take risks. It's true these risks can put them in danger of being hurt."
Meg Cabot
The Boy Next Door

"What you risk reveals what you value."
Jeanette Winterson
Written on the Body

"And the day came when the risk to remain tight in a bud was more painful than the risk it took to blossom."
Anaïs Nin

"Risk! Risk anything! Care no more for the opinions of others, for those voices. Do the hardest thing on earth for you. Act for yourself. Face the truth."
Katherine Mansfield

Roles

"Nobody objects to a woman being a good writer or sculptor or geneticist if at the same time she manages to be a good wife, a good mother, good-looking, good-tempered, well-dressed, well-groomed, and unaggressive."

Marya Mannes

"I've yet to be on a campus where most women weren't worrying about some aspect of combining marriage, children, and a career. I've yet to find one where many men were worrying about the same thing."

Gloria Steinem

"Women are supposed to be very calm generally: but women feel just as men feel; they need exercise of their faculties and a field for their efforts as much as their brothers do; they suffer from too rigid a restraint, too absolute a stagnation, precisely as men would suffer; and it is narrow-minded in their more privileged fellow-creatures to say they ought to confine themselves to making puddings and knitting stockings, to playing on the piano and embroidering bags. It is thoughtless to condemn them, or laugh at them, if they seek to do more or learn more than custom has pronounced for their sex."

Charlotte Brontë
Jane Eyre

Sacrifice

"Grudge no expense, yield to no opposition and forget fatigue till, by the strength of prayer and sacrifice, the spirit of love overcomes."
Maria W Chapman

"In olden times, sacrifices were made at the altar, a practice which is still very much practised."
Helen Rowland

"If you're a woman there's always a good reason to put yourself last ... I sometimes feel that sacrifice is written into our genes. It sits right next to the Guilt Chromosome that we inherited from our mothers."
Allison Pearson
Good Housekeeping, June 2003

Satisfaction

"You can be pleased with nothing when you are not pleased with yourself."
Lady Mary Wortley Montagu

"Nothing is more pleasing and engaging than the sense of having conferred benefits. Not even the gratification of receiving them."
Ellis Peters

"Look at a day when you are supremely satisfied at the end. It's not a day when you lounge around doing nothing; it's when you've had everything to do, and you've done it."
Margaret Thatcher

Security

"Security is mostly a superstition. It does not exist in nature … Life is either a daring adventure or nothing."
Helen Keller
The Open Door

"*Whether you're married or not, whether you have a boyfriend or not, there is no real security except for whatever you build inside yourself.*"
Gilda Radner

"Security is not the meaning of my life. Great opportunities are worth the risks."
Shirley Hufsteddler

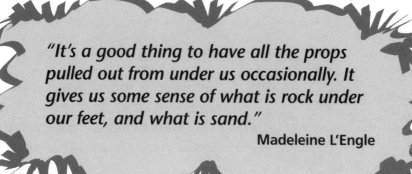

"It's a good thing to have all the props pulled out from under us occasionally. It gives us some sense of what is rock under our feet, and what is sand."

Madeleine L'Engle

Self

"What you are is a question only you can answer."

Lois McMaster Bujold
The Warrior's Apprentice

"Our deeds travel with us from afar, and we know what we have been makes us what we are."

George Eliot

"I would have girls regard themselves not as adjectives but as nouns."

Elizabeth Cady Stanton
Our Girls

"No woman wants to see herself too clearly."

Mignon McLaughlin
The Second Neurotic's Notebook

"Listening to other people's ideas about who you are can eat you up. Do they like me? Do they hate me? You could think about it all day long."

Reese Witherspoon

"Women are always being tested ... but ultimately, each of us has to define who we are individually and then do the very best job we can to grow into it."

Hillary Rodham Clinton

Self-acceptance

"I define comfort as self-acceptance. When we finally learn that self-care begins and ends with ourselves, we no longer demand sustenance and happiness from others."

Jennifer Louden

"Love yourself first and everything else falls into line. You really have to love yourself to get anything done in this world."

Lucille Ball

"A strong, positive self-image is the best possible preparation for success."

Dr Joyce Brothers

"To say something nice about yourself; this is the hardest thing in the world for people to do. They'd rather take their clothes off."

Nancy Friday

"Don't try and be someone else. Be the best version of you – the you that you know you can be."

Fiona Harrold

"The more I like me, the less I want to pretend to be other people."

Jamie Lee Curtis

"A human being is only interesting if he's in contact with himself. I learned you have to trust yourself, be what you are, and do what you ought to do the way you should do it. You have got to discover you, what you do, and trust it."

Barbra Streisand

"The thing that is really hard, and really amazing, is giving up on being perfect and beginning the work of becoming yourself."

Anna Quindlen

Self-control

"To enjoy freedom we have to control ourselves."

Virginia Woolf

"The sign of intelligent people is their ability to control emotions by the application of reason."

Marya Mannes

Self-development

"Like gaining confidence, finding one's courage is gradual rather than all at once."
Barbara Barksdale Clowse

"Yesterday I dared to struggle. Today I dare to win."
Bernadette Devlin

"Life's challenges are not supposed to paralyse you; they're supposed to help you discover who you are."
Bernice Johnson Reagon

"I want to be all that I am capable of becoming."
Katherine Mansfield

"You don't make progress by standing on the sidelines, whimpering and complaining. You make progress by implementing ideas."
Shirley Hufsteddler

"To create a larger vision for your life, you need to identify how you would most want to improve the quality of life for others."
Cheryl Richardson

"When you know better, you do better."
Maya Angelou

"In the long run, we shape our lives, and we shape ourselves. The process never ends until we die. And the choices we make are ultimately our own responsibility."

Eleanor Roosevelt

Self-discovery

"Self-discovery is the secret ingredient that fuels daring."
Grace Lichtenstein

"There's always someone to tell you you have to. Wrong. Don't. Rather, spend time finding out who you really are. Work on being more of that."
Shirley Jones
in *Success Secrets of Super-Achievers*

Self-esteem

"Don't worry so much about your self-esteem. Worry more about your character. Integrity is its own reward."
Laura Schlessinger

"The very thing we need to build a strong foundation of confidence and self-esteem is so simple – we need to spend time with ourselves."
Cheryl Richardson

> *"Self-esteem must be earned! When you dare to dream, dare to follow that dream, dare to suffer through the pain, sacrifice, self-doubts, and friction from the world, you will genuinely impress yourself."*
> **Laura Schlessinger**

Self-knowledge

"There's a period of life when we swallow a knowledge of ourselves and it becomes either good or sour inside."

Pearl Bailey

"We're constantly being told what other people think we are, and that's why it is so important to know yourself."
Sarah McLachlan

"To know yourself, to know that what you are doing is right, and to live with your own conscience is all that is necessary in life."

Mamie Doud Eisenhower

Self-pity

"Self-pity is our worst enemy and if we yield to it, we can never do anything wise in the world."
Helen Keller

"Never feel self-pity, the most destructive emotion there is. How awful to be caught up in the terrible squirrel cage of self."
Millicent Fenwick

"Life is to be lived. If you have to support yourself, you had better find some way that is going to be interesting. And you don't do that by sitting around wondering about yourself."
Katharine Hepburn

Self-respect

"True self-respect, being very different from false pride, leads inevitably to respecting others."
Virginia Moore
Virginia is a State of Mind

"Self-love has very little to do with how you feel about your outer self. It's about accepting all of yourself. You've got to learn to accept the fool in you as well as the part that's got it going on."
Tyra Banks

Service

"If you honour and serve the people who work for you, they will honour and serve you."

Mary Kay Ash

"Service comes best from those who are fulfilling their own talents and capacities, not by meekly accepting an externally imposed agenda."

Claire Foster

"Long hours that might mean love or neglect", *Church Times*, 17 October 2003

"Christ has no body now on earth but yours, no hands but yours, no feet but yours; yours are the eyes through which to look out Christ's compassion to the world, yours are the feet with which he is to go about doing good, and yours are the hands with which he is to bless us now."

St Teresa of Avila

Sex

"In America sex is an obsession; in other parts of the world it is a fact."

Marlene Dietrich

"To me, 'sexual freedom' means freedom from having to have sex."

Lily Tomlin

There is no remedy for sex but more sex.

Anon

"If women can sleep their way to the top, how come they aren't there? ... There must be an epidemic of insomnia out there."

Ellen Goodman

HOUSEWORK

Mary was married to a male chauvinist. They both worked full time, but he never did anything around the house and certainly not any housework. That, he declared, was woman's work!

But one evening Mary arrived home from work to find the children bathed, a load of washing in the washing machine and another in the dryer, dinner in the oven and a beautifully set table, complete with flowers. She was astonished, and she immediately wanted to know what was going on.

It turned out that Charley, her husband, had read a magazine article that suggested working wives would be more romantically inclined if they weren't so tired from having to do all the housework, in addition to holding down a full-time job.

The next day, she couldn't wait to tell her girlfriends at the office.

"How did it work out?" they asked.

"Well, it was a great dinner," Mary said. "And Charley even cleaned up, helped the kids with their homework, folded the laundry and put everything away. I really enjoyed my evening."

"But what about afterwards?" her friends wanted to know.

"It didn't work out," Mary said. "Charley was too tired."

Shoes

"I remember when I first bought my pointy kitten-heel sling-backs, feeling half amused and half shifty at the borrowed air of confidence that arrived when I put them on, and went away again as soon as I took them off."

Jane Shilling
The Times, 20 June 2003

If the shoe fits … get another one just like it.

The best way to forget all your troubles … is to wear really tight shoes.

"Confidence is … gorgeous shoes."
Woman & Home, June 2003

"What's the point of having lovely shoes if you've got ugly feet?"

Lesley Thomas
Telegraph Weekend, 21 June 2003

"I love the way heels make your legs look more elegant … and I love the poise and discipline that they give you … they force you to make more of an effort with every aspect of your appearance."
Sophie Ellis-Bextor
Sunday Telegraph Magazine, 28 December 2003

Signs

Some people write the funniest things:

Sign in a laundromat:
   "Automatic washing machines: please remove all your clothes when the light goes out"

Sign in a London department store:
   "Bargain basement upstairs"

In an office:
"**Would the person who took the step ladder yesterday please bring it back or further steps will be taken**"

Outside a farm:
"**Horse manure: 50p per pre-packed bag, 20p do-it-yourself**"

In an office:
"**After tea-break staff should empty the teapot and stand upside down on the draining board**"

On a church door:
"**This is the gate of heaven. Enter ye all by this door (This door is kept locked because of the draft. Please use side door)**"

English sign in a German café:
"**Mothers, Please Wash Your Hans Before Eating**"

Outside a secondhand shop:
"**We exchange anything – bicycles, washing machines etc. Why not bring your wife along and get a wonderful bargain?**"

Sign outside a new town hall which was to be opened by the Prince of Wales:
"**The town hall is closed until opening. It will remain closed after being opened. Open tomorrow**"

Outside a photographer's studio:
"**Out to lunch: if not back by five, out for dinner also**"

Seen at the side of a Sussex road:
"**Slow cattle crossing. No overtaking for the next 100 yrs.**"

Outside a disco:
"**Smarts is the most exclusive disco in town. Everyone welcome**"

Sign warning of quicksand:
"**Quicksand. Any person passing this point will be drowned. By order of the District Council**"

Notice sent to residents of a Wiltshire parish:

"Due to increasing problems with litter louts and vandals we must ask anyone with relatives buried in the graveyard to do their best to keep them in order"

Notice in a dry cleaner's window:

"Anyone leaving their garments here for more than 30 days will be disposed of"

Sign on motorway garage:

"Please do not smoke near our petrol pumps. Your life may not be worth much, but our petrol is"

Notice in health food shop window:

"Closed due to illness"

Spotted in a safari park:

"Elephants please stay in your car"

Seen during a conference:

"For anyone who has children and doesn't know it: there is a day care on the first floor"

Notice in a field:

"The farmer allows walkers to cross the field for free, but the bull charges"

Message on a leaflet:

"If you cannot read, this leaflet will tell you how to get lessons"

Sign on a repair shop door:

"We can repair anything (please knock hard on the door – the bell doesn't work)"

Sign at a Norfolk farm gate:

"Beware! I shoot every tenth trespasser and the ninth one has just left"

Spotted in a toilet in a London office block:

"Toilet out of order. Please use floor below"

More signs:

On a plumber's truck:
"We repair what your husband fixed"

Sign over a gynaecologist's office:
"Dr Jones, at your cervix"

On the trucks of a local plumbing company in north-east Pennsylvania:
"Don't sleep with a drip. Call your plumber"

Pizza shop slogan:
"7 days without pizza makes one weak"

Door of a plastic surgeon's office:
"Hello. Can we pick your nose?"

At a towing company:
"We don't charge an arm and a leg. We want tows"

On an electrician's truck:
"Let us remove your shorts"

In a non-smoking area:
"If we see smoke, we will assume you are on fire and take appropriate action"

On a maternity room door:
"Push, push, push"

At an optometrist's office:
"If you don't see what you're looking for, you've come to the right place"

On a taxidermist's window:
"We really know our stuff"

In a podiatrist's office:
"Time wounds all heels"

On a fence:
"Salesmen welcome! Dog food is expensive"

In a veterinarian's waiting room:
"Be back in five minutes. Sit! Stay!"

At the electric company:
"We would be de-lighted if you send in your bill. However, if you don't, you will be"

Silence

"Only when the clamour of the outside world is silenced will you be able to hear the deeper vibration. Listen carefully."

Sarah Ban Breathnach

"Arranging a bowl of flowers in the morning can give a sense of quiet in a crowded day – like writing a poem, or saying a prayer."

Anne Morrow Lindbergh

Simplicity

"It is always the simple that produces the marvellous."

Amelia E Barr

I Resign!

I am hereby officially tendering my resignation as an adult. I have decided I would like to accept the responsibilities of an eight-year-old again.

I want to go to McDonald's and think that it's a four-star restaurant.

I want to sail sticks across a fresh mud puddle and make an island with rocks.

I want to think M&Ms are better than money because you can eat them.

I want to lie under a big oak tree and run a lemonade stand with my friends on a hot summer's day.

I want to return to a time when life was simple: when all you knew were colours, multiplication tables, and nursery rhymes, but that didn't bother you, because you didn't know what you didn't know and you didn't care. All you knew was to be happy because you were blissfully unaware of all the things that should make you worried or upset.

I want to think the world is fair, that everyone is honest and good.

I want to believe that anything is possible.

I want to be oblivious to the complexities of life and be overly excited by the little things again.

I want to live simply again. I don't want my day to consist of computer crashes, mountains of paperwork, depressing news, how to survive more days in the month than there is money in the bank, doctor bills, gossip, illness, and loss of loved ones.

I want to believe in the power of smiles, hugs, a kind word, truth, justice, peace, dreams, the imagination, mankind, and making angels in the snow.

So ... here's my chequebook and my car keys, my credit card bills and my storecards. I am officially resigning from adulthood. And if you want to discuss this further, you'll have to catch me first, 'cause "Tag! You're it."

Sisters

"The best thing about having a sister was that I always had a friend."

Cali Rae Turner

"Sister is probably the most competitive relationship within the family, but once the sisters are grown, it becomes the strongest relationship."

Margaret Mead

"Women are in league with each other, a secret conspiracy of hearts and pheromones."

Camille Paglia

"We are all sisters under the flesh."

Sylvia Gonzales

Sleep

Better to get up late and be wide awake than to get up early and be asleep all day.

Anon

"A ruffled mind makes a restless pillow."

Charlotte Brontë

"No day is so bad it can't be fixed with a nap."

Carrie Snow

Smile

"I have witnessed the softening of the hardest of hearts by a simple smile."
Goldie Hawn

"People who keep stiff upper lips find that it's damn hard to smile."
Judith Guest

"A smile is an instant face-lift."
Dayle Haddon

"Smile at each other, smile at your wife, smile at your husband, smile at your children, smile at each other – it doesn't matter who it is – and that will help you to grow up in greater love for each other."
Mother Teresa

Solitude

"Inside myself is a place where I live all alone and that's where you renew your springs that never dry up."
Pearl S Buck

"It is important from time to time to slow down, to go away by yourself, and simply be."
Eileen Caddy

"Solitude is the human condition in which I keep myself company. Loneliness comes about when I am alone without being able to split up into the two-in-one, without being able to keep myself company."

Hannah Arendt

"Women need real moments of solitude and self-reflection to balance out how much of ourselves we give away."

Barbara De Angelis

"Solitude is such a potential thing. We hear voices in solitude, we never hear in the hurry and turmoil of life; we receive counsels and comforts, we get under no other condition."

Amelia E Barr

"One can acquire everything in solitude – except character."

Marie Henri Beyle

"We need quiet time to examine our lives openly and honestly ... spending quiet time alone gives your mind an opportunity to renew itself and create order."

Susan Taylor

"There is a solitude which each and every one of us has always carried within. More inaccessible than the ice cold mountains, more profound than the midnight sea: the solitude of self."

Elizabeth Cady Stanton

Sorrow

"I can't think of any sorrow in the world that a hot bath wouldn't help, just a little bit."
Susan Glasee
The Visioning

"How small and selfish is sorrow. But it bangs one about until one is senseless."
Elizabeth, the Queen Mother

"There is alchemy in sorrow. It can be transmuted into wisdom, which, if it does not bring joy, can yet bring happiness."
Pearl S Buck

Stereotyping

"At the same time we tell girls they can do anything and be anything, we tell them, 'You'd better be really thin. And you'd better be tall. And you'd better be super-organised so you can do a million things at once.' We give all of these messages that undermine individuality, instead of saying, 'Be the best person you can be.'"
Hillary Rodham Clinton

"The emotional, sexual, and psychological stereotyping of females begins when the doctor says, 'It's a girl.'"
Shirley Chisholm

"We must reject not only stereotypes that others hold of us, but also the stereotypes we hold of ourselves."
Shirley Chisholm

Strength

"Women are never stronger than when they arm themselves with their weakness."
Marie de Vichy-Chamrond
Letters to Voltaire

"Toughness doesn't have to come in a pinstriped suit."
Senator Dianne Feinstein

Stress

"Stress is basically a disconnection from the earth, a forgetting of the breath. Stress is an ignorant state. It believes that everything is an emergency. Nothing is that important. Just lie down."
Natalie Goldberg

"No matter how much pressure you feel at work, if you could find ways to relax for at least five minutes every hour, you'd be more productive."
Dr Joyce Brothers

Stress is when your cope runneth over.

"Tranquilisers only work if you follow the advice on the bottle: Keep away from children."
Phyllis Diller

"Throw out an alarming alarm clock. If the ring is loud and strident, you're waking up to instant stress. You shouldn't be bullied out of bed, just reminded that it's time to start your day."
Sharon Gold

Struggle

"When you struggle, that's when you realise what you're made of, and that's when you realise what the people around you can do. You learn who you'd want to take with you to a war, and who you'd only want to take to lunch."
Chamique Holdsclaw

"If nothing in life is a struggle then life itself will become one."
Britt Etters

Success

"Ultimately, the most vital ingredient in success is believing that you will succeed."
Sharon Maxwell Magnus
Radio Times, 4–10 October 2003

"The penalty of success is to be bored by people who used to snub you."
Lady Nancy Astor

"To follow, without halt, one aim: that's the secret of success."
Anna Pavlova

"My quirkiness is what's made me successful."
Toyah Wilcox
Good Housekeeping,
September 2003

"The only thing that separates successful people from the ones who aren't is the willingness to work very, very hard."

Helen Gurley Brown

"I've never sought success in order to get fame and money; it's the talent and the passion that count in success."

Ingrid Bergman

"Success is liking yourself, liking what you do, and liking how you do it."

Maya Angelou

"Behind every successful woman is herself – look after her, she needs your support."

Allison Pearson
"Sacrifice is Written in our Genes", *Good Housekeeping*, June 2003

"My private measure of success is daily. If this were to be the last day of my life would I be content with it? To live in a harmonious balance of commitments and pleasures is what I strive for."

Jane Rule

"Success is the satisfaction of feeling that one is realising one's ideal."

Anna Pavlova

Suffering

"One feels friendly towards all who are suffering in the same way as oneself."

Nan Le Ruez
"Dear Diary", *Saga*, August 2003

"One does not love a place the less for having suffered in it, unless it has all been suffering, nothing but suffering."

Jane Austen

"Sorrow or trial lovingly submitted to does not prevent our being happy – it rather purifies the happiness."

Mary Mackillop

"So long as little children are allowed to suffer, there is no true love in this world."

Isodore Duncan

Survival

"Knowing when to stop is one of the secrets of survival ... and knowing when not to."

Elizabeth Buchan
The Good Wife

"Only the insane hope to be permanently happy. Sad things happen and whether you either survive well or survive badly, it's up to you."

Sheila Hancock
interview, Radio Times, 13–19 December 2003

"I survived because I was tougher than anyone else."

Bette Davis
(commenting on her career at age 66)

Talent

"Talent, like beauty, to be pardoned, must be obscure and unostentatious."
Marguerite Gardiner

"We cannot take credit for our talents. It is how we use our talents that counts."
Madeleine L'Engle

"God would not give us the same talents if what were right for men were wrong for women."
Sarah Orne Jewett

"A career is born in public, talent in privacy."
Marilyn Monroe

"Genius is the gold in the mine; talent is the miner that works and brings it out."
Marguerite, Lady Blessington

"All our talents increase in the using, and every faculty, both good and bad, strengthens by exercise."
Anne Brontë

Talk

Great people talk about great ideas; average people talk about average ideas; small people talk about other people.

Anon

"A closed mouth gathers no foot."
Julie Andrews

"Much talking is the cause of danger. Silence is the means of avoiding misfortune. The talkative parrot is shut up in a cage. Other birds, without speech, fly freely about."
Saskya Pandita

Thankfulness

"Every time we remember to say 'thank you', we experience nothing less than heaven on earth."
Sarah Ban Breathnach

"We are all more blind to what we have than to what we have not."
Audre Lord

Thinking

"The trouble with most people is that they think with their hopes or fears or wishes rather than with their minds."
Lady Nancy Astor

"Readers are plentiful; thinkers are rare."
Harriet Martineau

"Never be afraid to sit awhile and think."
Lorraine Hansberry

"Sloppy thinking gets worse over time."
Jenny Holzer

"Walking is also an ambulation of mind."
Gretel Ehrlich

"People do not like to think. If one thinks, one must reach conclusions. Conclusions are not always pleasant."
Helen Keller

Time

"We say we waste time, but that is impossible. We waste ourselves."
Alice Bloch

Time is like a snowflake – it melts away while we try to decide what to do with it.
Anon

"I must govern the clock, not be governed by it."
Golda Meir

"Spend the afternoon: you can't take it with you."
Annie Dillard
Pilgrim at Tinker Creek

"Time is the thief you cannot banish."
Phyllis McGinley

"Nothing cures like time and love."
Laura Nyro

"We need time to dream, time to remember, and time to reach the infinite. Time to be."
Gladys Taber

"There is a time for work and a time for love. That leaves no other time."
Coco Chanel

"How long a minute is depends on what side of the bathroom door you're on. Just as you began to feel that you could make good use of time, there was no time left to you."
Lisa Alther

"Time is a cruel thief to rob us of our former selves. We lose as much to life as we do to death."
Elizabeth Forsythe Hailey
A Woman of Independent Means

Today

Today

Today, when I awoke, I suddenly realised that this is the best day of my life, ever! There were times when I wondered if I would make it to today … but I did! And because I did, I'm going to celebrate!

Today, I'm going to celebrate what a great life I have had so far; the accomplishments, the many blessings, and even the hardships, because they have served to make me stronger.

I will go through this day with my head held high, and a happy heart. I will marvel at God's seemingly simple gifts: the morning dew, the sun, the clouds, the trees, the flowers, the birds. Today, none of these miraculous creations will escape my notice.

Today, I will share my excitement for life with other people. I'll make someone smile. I'll go out of my way to perform an unexpected act of kindness for someone I don't even know.

Today, I'll give a sincere compliment to someone who seems down. I'll tell a child how special he is, and I'll tell someone I love just how deeply I care for her, and how much she means to me.

Today is the day I quit worrying about what I don't have, and start being grateful for all the wonderful things God has already given me. I'll remember that to worry is just a waste of time, because my faith in God and his plan ensures everything will be just fine.

And tonight, before I go to bed, I'll go outside and raise my eyes to the heavens. I will stand in awe at the beauty of the stars and the moon, and I will praise God for these magnificent treasures.

As the day ends and I lay my head down on my pillow, I will thank the Almighty for the best day of my life. And I will sleep the sleep of a contented child, excited with expectation because I know tomorrow is going to be the best day of my life, ever!

Source unknown

"You better live your best and act your best and think your best today, for today is the sure preparation for tomorrow and all the other tomorrows that follow."
Harriet Martineau

"I live a day at a time. Each day I look for a kernel of excitement. In the morning I say: 'What is my exciting thing for today?' Then, I do the day. Don't ask me about tomorrow."
Barbara Jordan

Tradition

"Traditions are the guideposts driven deep in our subconscious minds. The most powerful ones are those we can't even describe, aren't even aware of."
Ellen Goodman

"Traditions are group efforts to keep the unexpected from happening."
Barbara Tober

"No written law has ever been more binding than unwritten custom supported by popular opinion."
Carrie Chapman Catt

Travel

"Certainly, travel is more than the seeing of sights; it is a change that goes on, deep and permanent, in the ideas of living."

Miriam Beard
Realism in Romantic Japan

"My favourite thing is to go where I've never been."
Diane Arbus

"The impulse to travel is one of the hopeful symptoms of life."

Agnes Repplier
"The American Takes a Holiday",
Time and Tendencies

"Trips do not end when you return home – usually this is the time when in a sense they really begin."
Agnes E Benedict and **Adele Franklin**
The Happy Home

Signs You've Chosen a "No Frills" Airline

You can't board the plane unless you have the exact change.

The captain asks all the passengers to chip in towards the fuel.

Before you take off, the flight attendant tells you to fasten your Velcro.

When they pull the steps away, the plane starts rocking.

The captain yells at the ground crew to get the cows off the runway.

You ask the captain how often their planes crash and he says, "Just once".

No movie. Don't need one. Your life keeps flashing before your eyes.

You see a man with a gun, but he's demanding to be let off the plane.

All the planes have both a bathroom and a chapel.

"*Perhaps travel cannot prevent bigotry, but by demonstrating that all peoples cry, laugh, eat, worry, and die, it can introduce the idea that if we try to understand each other, we may even become friends.*"

Maya Angelou
"Passports to Understanding",
Wouldn't Take Nothing for My Journey Now

Trust

It takes years to build up trust, but only seconds to destroy it.

Anon

"I trust life not because I trust the world, but because I trust the God who lives in my heart."
Marianne Williamson

"Creativity comes from trust. Trust your instincts."
Rita Mae Brown

"*I've learned to trust myself, to listen to truth, to not be afraid of it and to not try and hide it.*"
Sarah McLachlan

"Never trust a husband too far, nor a bachelor too near."
Helen Rowland

Truth

"The facts are always less than what really happened."
Nadine Gordimer

"Legend remains victorious in spite of history."
Sarah Bernhardt

"Nobody speaks the truth when there's something they must have."
Elizabeth Bowen

"Truth has beauty, power and necessity."
Sylvia Ashton-Warner

"The truth is always exciting. Speak it, then. Life is dull without it."
Pearl S Buck

"It is in our idleness, in our dreams, that submerged truth sometimes comes to the top."
Virginia Woolf
A Room of One's Own

"Truth, though it has many disadvantages, is at least changeless. You can always find it where you left it."
Phyllis Bottome
Under the Skin

"Most of the basic truths of life sound absurd at first hearing."
Elizabeth Goudge

"You never find yourself until you face the truth."
Pearl Bailey

"Truth is the only safe ground to stand on."
Elizabeth Cady Stanton

"Truth isn't always beauty, but the hunger for it is."
Nadine Gordimer

Uncertainty

"If we can recognise that change and uncertainty are basic principles, we can greet the future and the transformation we are undergoing with the understanding that we do not know enough to be pessimistic."

Hazel Henderson

"Tolerance of uncertainty is a measure of maturity … and a sign of how much you value and accept yourself."

Dr Dorothy Rowe
Woman & Home, June 2003

"The only thing that makes life possible is permanent, intolerable uncertainty; not knowing what comes next."
Ursula K LeGuin

Victim

"All of us are, to some extent, victims of what we are. We are not limited by our imaginations, but by our ability to do what we imagine. We are not too often limited by our abilities as much as by circumstances. And we are not as often limited by our circumstances as much as by the lack of the will to respond."

Dee Bowman
That's Life!

"You are a victim of the rules you live by."
Jenny Holzer

Vision

"A vision is not just a picture of what could be; it is an appeal to our better selves, a call to become something more."

Rosabeth Moss Kanter

"Visions come not to polluted eyes."
Mary Howitt

"To look backward for a while is to refresh the eye, to restore it, and to render it the more fit for its prime function of looking forward."
Margaret Fairless Barber

War

"War is not its own end, except in some catastrophic slide into absolute damnation. It's peace that's wanted. Some better peace than the one you started with."

Lois McMaster Bujold
The Vor Game

War never decided who was right, only who was left.

Anon

"Women might start a rumour, but not a war."

Marga Gomez

"The worst barbarity of war is that it forces men collectively to commit acts against which individually they would revolt with their whole being."

Ellen Key

"People who talk about peace are very often the most quarrelsome."

Lady Nancy Astor

"War is not nice."
Barbara Bush

Weakness

"Our strength is often composed of the weaknesses we're damned if we're going to show."
Mignon McLaughlin

"Let us look at our shortcomings and leave other people's alone ... There is no reason why we should expect everyone else to travel by our road."
St Teresa of Avila

"I think what weakens people most is fear of wasting their strength."
Etty Hillesum
An Interrupted Life

Wealth

"They say it is better to be poor and happy than rich and miserable, but how about a compromise like moderately rich and just moody?"
Princess Diana

"I have no riches but my thoughts, yet these are wealth enough for me."
Sarah J Hale

"Being rich is having money; being wealthy is having time."
Margaret Bonnano

"Abundance is, in large part, an attitude."
Sue Patton Thoele

"It is not the creation of wealth that is wrong, but the love of money for its own sake."
Margaret Thatcher

Why

Why is the third hand on the watch called the "second hand"?

Why do we say something is "out of whack"? What is a whack?

Why do "slow down" and "slow up" mean the same thing?

Why do "fat chance" and "slim chance" mean the same thing?

Why do "tug" boats *push* their barges?

Why are they called "stands" when they are made for sitting?

Why is it called "after dark" when it really is "after light"?

Why are a "wise man" and a "wise guy" opposites?

Why do "overlook" and "oversee" mean opposite things?

Why is "phonics" not spelled the way it sounds?

Why is "bra" singular and "panties" plural?

Why do you press harder on the buttons of a remote control when you know the batteries are dead?

Why do we put suits in garment bags and garments in a suitcase?

Why do we wash bath towels? Aren't we clean when we use them?

Why doesn't glue stick to the inside of the bottle?

Why do they call it a TV "set" when you only have one?

If a word is misspelled in the dictionary, how would we ever know?

If Webster wrote the first dictionary, where did he find the words?

If work is so terrific, why do they have to pay you to do it?

If all the world is a stage, where is the audience sitting?

If love is blind, why is lingerie so popular?

If you are cross-eyed and have dyslexia, can you read all right?

Winning

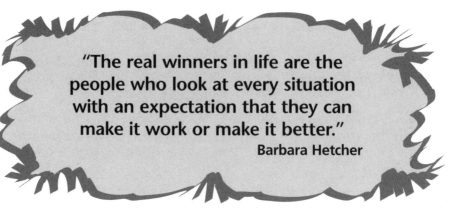

"The real winners in life are the people who look at every situation with an expectation that they can make it work or make it better."

Barbara Hetcher

"Often the best way to win is to forget to keep score."

Mariane Espinosa Murphy

"You can stand tall without standing on someone. You can be a victor without having victims."

Harriet Woods

"You're not obligated to win. You're obligated to keep trying to do the best you can every day."
Marian Wright Edelman

Wisdom

"Never mistake knowledge
for wisdom. One helps you
make a living; the other
helps you make a life."
Sandra Carey

"Being wise is not
believing everything
you think."
Donna A Favors

*Wisdom
is scar tissue
in disguise.*
Anon

*"Wisdom is not acquired
save as the result of
investigation."*
Sara Teasdale

*"To acquire knowledge, one
must study; but to acquire
wisdom, one must observe."*
Marilyn vos Savant

*"A wise woman puts a grain of
sugar into everything she says to a
man, and takes a grain of salt with
everything he says to her."*
Helen Rowland

Woman

> "Today's woman of faith may not be able to have it all – at least, not all at once, but, like her sisters in the past, present and future, she has the power to fulfil her God-given potential and change the world in ways he always knew we would."
>
> **Michelle Guinness**
> *Woman: The Full Story*

> "I am a woman above everything else."
> Jacqueline Kennedy Onassis

Reasons Eve Was Created

God was worried that Adam would frequently become lost in the garden because he would not ask for directions.

God knew that one day Adam would require someone to locate and hand him the remote.

God knew Adam would never go out and buy himself a new fig leaf when his wore out and would therefore need Eve to buy one for him.

God knew Adam would never be able to make a doctor's, dentist's, or haircut appointment for himself.

God knew Adam would never remember which night to put the wheelie bin out.

God knew if the world was to be populated, men would never be able to handle the pain and discomfort of childbearing.

As the Keeper of the Garden, Adam would never remember where he left his tools.

Apparently, Adam needed someone to blame his troubles on when God caught him hiding in the garden.

As the Bible says, it is not good for man to be alone!

"I should like to know what is the proper function of women, if it is not to make reasons for husbands to stay at home, and still stronger reasons for bachelors to go out."
George Eliot
The Mill on the Floss

"Women are one of the Almighty's enigmas to prove to men that he knows more than they do."
Ellen Glasgow

Words

Wonderful Words

Arbitrator *ar'-bi-tray-ter*\\: A cook that leaves Arby's to work at McDonald's.

Avoidable *uh-voy'-duh-buhl*\\: What a bullfighter tries to do.

Baloney *buh-lo'-nee*\\: Where some hemlines fall.

Bernadette *burn'-a-det*\\: The act of torching a mortgage.

Burglarise *bur'-gler-ize*\\: What a crook sees with.

Control *kon-trol'*\\: A short, ugly inmate.

Counterfeiters *kown-ter-fit-ers*\\: Workers who put together kitchen cabinets.

Eyedropper *i'-drop-ur*\\: A clumsy ophthalmologist.

Burglarize →

Heroes *hee'-rhos*\: What a guy in a boat does.

Left Bank *left' bangk'*\: What the robber did when his bag was full of loot.

Misty *mis'-tee*\: How golfers create divots.

Paradox *par'-u-doks*\: Two physicians.

Parasites *par'-uh-sites*\: What you see from the top of the Eiffel Tower.

Pharmacist *farm'-uh-sist*\: A helper on the farm.

Polarise *po'-lur-ize*\: What penguins see with.

Primate *pri'-mat*\: Removing your spouse from in front of the TV.

Relief *ree-leef'*\: What trees do in the spring.

Rubberneck *rub'-er-nek*\: What you do to relax your wife.

Seamstress *seem'-stres*\: Describes 12 stone in a size 10.

Selfish *sel'-fish*\: What the owner of a seafood store does.

Subdued *sub-dyood'*\: Like, a guy, like, works on one of those, like, submarines, man.

"You can taste a word."
Pearl Bailey

"I like good strong words that mean something."
Louisa May Alcott
Little Women

"We have too many high-sounding words, and too few actions that correspond with them."
Abigail Adams
letter to John Adams, 1774

"For your born writer, nothing is so healing as the realisation that he has come upon the right word."
Catherine Drinker Bowen

Be careful of the words you say,
Keep them short and sweet.
You never know, from day to day,
Which ones you'll have to eat.
Anon

"For me, words are a form of action, capable of influencing change."
Ingrid Bengis

The six most important words: I admit I made a mistake
The five most important words: You did a good job
The four most important words: What is your opinion?
The three most important words: If you please
The two most important words: Thank you
The one least important word: I

Anon

"Kind words can be short and easy to speak, but their echoes are truly endless."
Mother Teresa

"Once you can express yourself, you can tell the world what you want from it ... All the changes in the world, for good or evil, were first brought about by words."
Jacqueline Kennedy Onassis

Top 25 Oxymorons

Exact estimate
Act naturally
Found missing
Resident alien
Genuine imitation
Airline food
Good grief
Government organisation
Alone together
Small crowd
Business ethics
Soft rock
Sweet sorrow
"Now, then … "
Passive aggression
Clearly misunderstood
Extinct life
Plastic glasses
Terribly pleased
Tight slacks
Definite maybe
Pretty ugly
Working vacation
Religious tolerance
Microsoft Works
… and don't anyone dare add "Women's wisdom".

Words Women Use – A Guide for Men

"Fine"
This is the word women use to end an argument when they feel they are right and you need to shut up. Never use "fine" to describe how a woman looks; this will cause you to have one of those arguments.

"Five Minutes"
This is half an hour. It is equivalent to the five minutes that your football game is going to last before you take out the dustbin, so it's a fair trade.

"Nothing"
This means "Something", and you should be on your toes. "Nothing" is usually used to describe the feeling a woman has of wanting to turn you inside out, upside down, and backwards. "Nothing" usually signifies an argument that will last "Five Minutes" and end with "Fine".

"Go Ahead" (with raised eyebrows)
This is a dare. One that will result in a woman getting upset over "Nothing" and will end with the word "Fine".

"Go Ahead" (normal eyebrows)
This means "I give up" or "Do what you want because I don't care". You will get a "Raised Eyebrow Go Ahead" in just a few minutes, followed by "Nothing" and "Fine" and she will talk to you in about "Five Minutes" when she cools off.

"Loud Sigh"
This is not actually a word, but is a non-verbal statement often misunderstood by men. A "Loud Sigh" means she thinks you are an idiot at that moment, and wonders why she is wasting her time standing here and arguing with you over "Nothing".

"Soft Sigh"
Again, not a word, but a non-verbal statement. "Soft Sighs" mean that she is content. Your best bet is to not move or breathe, and she will stay content.

"That's OK"
This is one of the most dangerous statements that a woman can make to a man. "That's OK" means that she wants to think long and hard before paying you back for whatever it is that you have done. "That's OK" is often used with the word "Fine" and in conjunction with a "Raised Eyebrow".

"Go Ahead"
At some point in the near future, you are going to be in some mighty big trouble.

"Please Do"
This is not a statement; it is an offer. A woman is giving you the chance to come up with whatever excuse or reason you have for doing whatever it is that you have done. You have a fair chance with the truth, so be careful and you shouldn't get a "That's OK".

"Thanks"
A woman is thanking you. Do not faint. Just say, "You're welcome".

"Thanks a Lot"
This is much different from "Thanks". A woman will say, "Thanks A Lot" when she is really annoyed with you. It signifies that you have offended her in some callous way, and will be followed by the "Loud Sigh". Be careful not to ask what is wrong after the "Loud Sigh", as she will only tell you "Nothing".

Work

"You cannot be really first-rate at your work if your work is all you are."

Anna Quindlen
A Short Guide to a Happy Life

"Your work is the rent you pay for the room you occupy on earth."
Elizabeth, the Queen Mother

"You don't stop working because you grow old – you grow old because you stop working."
Dr Fanny Waterman
(in a radio interview, in which she said she was 83 and still working)

"I learned the value of hard work by working hard."

Margaret Mead

"I do not know anyone who has got to the top without hard work. That is the recipe. It will not always get you to the top, but should get you pretty near."

Margaret Thatcher

"Measure not the work until the day's out and the labour done."
Elizabeth Barrett Browning

"My professional life is completely dominated by men … the top executives are all men. There are a few women getting there, but not quite yet. But it will change … Here I am … there you are … it's not by accident."

Isabella Rossellini
Woman & Home, July 2003

"Work is either fun or drudgery. It depends on your attitude. I like fun."
Colleen C Barrett

"I have frequently been questioned, especially by women, of how I could reconcile family life with a scientific career. Well, it has not been easy."

Marie Curie

Lampner's Law of Employment:
When leaving work late, you will go unnoticed. When you leave work early, you will meet the boss in the car park.

"The trouble with working from home is that you have to re-invent yourself every morning ... from the motley jumble in the cupboard, all of which looks somehow too plain, too fancy, too sloppy, too smart – completely unsuitable for the image you want to project, whatever that may be."

Jane Shilling
The Times, 20 June 2003

Reasons to give up work

1. Because I have two lives and I don't have time to enjoy either of them.
2. Because 24 hours are not enough.
3. Because my children will be young for only a short time.
4. Because one day I caught my husband looking at me the way my mother used to look at my father.
5. Because becoming a man is a waste of a woman.
6. Because I am too tired to think of another because.

Allison Pearson
I Don't Know How She Does It

Translate Your Resumé

Outgoing Personality............Always going out of the office
Good Communication Skills........Spends lots of time on phone
Average Employee............Not too bright
Exceptionally Well-qualified..........Made no major blunders yet
Work is First Priority............Too ugly to get a date
Active Socially............Drinks a lot
Family is Active Socially............Spouse drinks, too
Independent Worker............Nobody knows what she does
Quick-thinking............Offers plausible excuses
Careful Thinker............Won't make a decision
Aggressive............Obnoxious
Uses Logic on Difficult Jobs............Gets someone else to do it
Expresses Themselves Well............Speaks English
Meticulous Attention to Detail............A nit-picker
Has Leadership Qualities............Is tall or has a loud voice
Exceptionally Good Judgement............Lucky
Keen Sense of Humour............Knows a lot of dirty jokes
Career-minded............Back-stabber
Loyal............Can't get a job anywhere else

Worry

"Worry a little every day and in a lifetime you will lose a couple of years. If something is wrong, fix it if you can. But train yourself not to worry. Worry never fixes anything."

Mary Hemingway

"If you can fix the thing that worries you, then fix it; otherwise don't waste precious time or energy on it."

Colleen Grant

Writers and Writing

"Writers should be read, but neither seen nor heard."

Daphne du Maurier

A writer lives in awe of words for they can be cruel or kind, and they can change their meanings right in front of you. They pick up flavours and odours like butter in a refrigerator.

Anon

"Nothing you write, if you hope to be good, will ever come out as you first hoped."
Lillian Hellman

"Writing is a solitary occupation. Family, friends, and society are the natural enemies of the writer. He must be alone, uninterrupted, and slightly savage if he is to sustain and complete an undertaking."

Jessamyn West

"Writing is making sense of life. You work your whole life and perhaps you've made sense of one small area."
Nadine Gordimer

"Writing is not at all easy, but it is interesting and rewarding."
Esther Rantzen
The Times, 15 July 2003

"If I had to give young writers advice, I would say: Don't listen to writers talking about writing or themselves."
Lillian Hellman

"Looking back, I imagine I was always writing. Twaddle it was too. But better far write twaddle or anything, anything, than nothing at all."
Katherine Mansfield

"I don't know much about creative writing programs. But they're not telling the truth if they don't teach, one, that writing is hard work, and, two, that you have to give up a great deal of life, your personal life, to be a writer."
Doris Lessing

Wrong

"Each wrong act brings with it its own aesthetic, dulling the conscience and blinding it against further light, and sometimes for years."

Rose Macaulay
Letters to a Friend

"Sin makes its own hell, and goodness its own heaven."
Mary Baker Eddy

Youth

"It is the fight itself that keeps you young."

Collette

"The dead might as well try to speak to the living as the old to the young."
Willa Cather

"To find joy in work is to discover the fountain of youth."
Pearl S Buck
The Joy of Children

"The secret of eternal youth is arrested development."
Alice Roosevelt Longworth

"It is not possible for civilisation to flow backward while there is youth in the world. Youth may be headstrong, but it will advance its allotted length."
Helen Keller

"There is nothing can pay one for that invaluable ignorance which is the companion of youth, those sanguine groundless hopes, and that lively vanity which makes all the happiness of life."
Lady Mary Wortley Montagu

"Youth is something very new: 20 years ago no one mentioned it."
Coco Chanel

The younger we are, the more we want to change the world. The older we are, the more we want to change the young.
Source unknown

Zeal

"I don't know about having too much zeal; but I think it is better the pot should boil over than not boil at all."

Source unknown

Index of themes